SPED
076

Kranes, Dr. Judith Eh...

The Hidden Handicap

THE
HIDDEN
HANDICAP

Helping the
Marginally Learning Disabled
from Infancy
to Young Adulthood

Dr. Judith Ehre Kranes

SIMON AND SCHUSTER

New York

DESIGNED BY EVE METZ
MANUFACTURED IN THE UNITED STATES OF AMERICA

1 2 3 4 5 6 7 8 9 10

LIBRARY OF CONGRESS CATALOGING IN PUBLICATION DATA

KRANES, JUDITH EHRE.
THE HIDDEN HANDICAP.

BIBLIOGRAPHY: P.
INCLUDES INDEX.
1. LEARNING DISABILITIES.   I. TITLE.
LC4704.K7   371.9'26   79-20641
ISBN 0-671-24242-3

THE CASE HISTORIES IN THIS BOOK ARE BASED ON COMBINATIONS
OF ACTUAL EXPERIENCES. NAMES AND IDENTIFYING CHARACTER-
ISTICS HAVE BEEN CHANGED IN ORDER TO MAINTAIN THE PRIVACY
OF THE INDIVIDUALS CONCERNED.

The author gratefully acknowledges permission to quote from the following:
  Motor development charts reprinted from *Caring for Children*, copyright
© 1975 by M. W. Draper and H. E. Draper. Used with permission of the
publisher, Chas. A. Bennett Co., Inc. All rights reserved.
  From *Childhood and Adolescence: A Psychology of the Growing Person*, 3rd
edition, by L. Joseph Stone and Joseph Church. Copyright © 1957, 1968 by
Random House, Inc., © 1972 by L. Joseph Stone and Joseph Church. Reprinted by permission of the publisher.

In Memory of
Sidney A. Kranes
Whose love for obscure seeds provided the earth
for my garden

Contents

CONTENTS

ACKNOWLEDGMENTS

It gives me great pleasure to express my appreciation of those individuals who, in one way or another, supported the work that enabled me to produce *The Hidden Handicap*.

I was extraordinarily fortunate to have the abiding support of Mrs. Louise Pinkerton Marshall, and the Pinkerton Foundation, with the help, particularly, of Miss Joan Colello and Mr. George Gillespie III, along with Mr. Thomas J. Sweeney, Jr., Mr. Robert Bach, Mr. David Fuchs, and Mrs. Marcia Warner, who are on the Para-Educator Foundation board of directors. In the very beginning of my work, before I dreamed of the possibility of the Para-Educator Center for Young Adults, I must single out Mr. Sweeney, Mr. Bach, and Miss Colello, for the first scholarship efforts on behalf of our Marginally Learning Disabled young adults; and to the entire generous-spirited group, there should be added The Louis Calder Foundation, for underwriting a number of fellowships for New York University doctoral students; through the Calder grants, they were able to study at PEC, thus enabling its work to spread beyond the walls of the university.

I am also grateful to the late Dr. Jesse Zizmor, whose dedication to the cause of the MLD drew me into its picture; Dr. Alfred Ellison, the former chairman of my university department, who was the first of my professional colleagues to appreciate the value of my experiment; and the School of Education deans, Daniel E. Griffiths, and John C. Payne, recently deceased, who gave the center its backing.

Additionally, there came the dedication of an exceptionally fine PEC staff, which has been essential to the program's success. It includes: Cynthia Bonnes, Louise Brown, Esther Conrad, Miriam Lawin, Irene Metzger, Joy Moser, Judith

Schwartz, Kathryn Schwyzer, Leo Shapiro, and Anne Wright. I was fortunate, too, to have the services of Mrs. Ella Berman, Administrative Assistant, who performs beyond any call of duty, and Mrs. Eleanor Lee, who helps the PEC wheels turn smoothly. Then, Drs. Larry Balter, Susan Frame, Ann Simon, Irving Steingart, and Lynne Atlas-Wittkin, the students' counselors, have increased the program's strength through their insights and devotion.

Indispensable to the success of the PEC venture, which led, as well, to *The Hidden Handicap*, are the teachers and directors of the cooperating schools. For those who had the courage to join in its pioneer effort, before it seemed worthwhile to do so, I give special thanks to the Little Red School House, Bank Street College Nursery School, City and Country School, Horace Mann School for Nursery Years, and the Temple Emanu-El Nursery School; with the expansion of the PEC population, the list happily adds All Souls Nursery School, Community Church Nursery School, Community House Nursery School, Corlears School, Fiedel School, Hudson Guild Head Start, Leonard Johnson School, Lincoln Square Synagogue Nursery School, Little Star of Broome Day Care, Merricat's Castle Nursery School, Midtown Emanu-El Nursery School, Morningside Head Start, 92nd Street YMHA/YWHA, Riverside Nursery-Kindergarten, St. Luke's Nursery School, and the Walden School. Midtown Emanu-El provided several of the children's quotations that appear in chapter 3.

Further, I want to express my gratitude to: Major John H. Lambert and Miss Opal Pierce—their support of our PEC students, who live at the Parkside, a nonsectarian residence run by the Salvation Army, has added a valuable dimension to their lives; Professor Esther Menaker, distinguished clinical psychologist, who gave me some of the benefits of her training, Professor Bluma Weiner, Department of Special Education, Yeshiva University, Dr. Larry Benjamin, Assistant Clinical Professor at Albert Einstein College of Medicine, Professor Leonard Diller, Chief of Behavioral Sciences at the Institute of Rehabilitation Medicine, New York University, and Dr. Barbara Biber, Professor, Bank Street College, who were the first professionals in the exceptional children field to listen to me; Professor Lillie Pope, Director, Psycho-Educational Center, Coney Island Hospital, who, on a couple of very important occasions, stepped forward with her expert advice and assistance; and the late Professor Daniel Ringelheim, who provided my first link with Mrs. Martha Bernard; initially Mrs. Bernard made it possible for me to reach the audiences connected with the Association for Children with Learning Disabilities. Her pioneering work in New York City, state and nationally, has been a boon for all concerned.

Finally, that the account of *The Hidden Handicap* finds itself in print, I owe, first, to my steadfast friend, Irvin Ehrenpreis, Linden Kent Professor of English at the University of Virginia, who pushed me to write it; and, secondly, to my editor, Jonathan Coleman, for his guidance and wisdom.

FOREWORD

In American culture we have long respected two ideas that do not always fit together very smoothly in practice. One of these ideas is the full development of each person to the limit of his or her abilities; and the other idea is selection by merit or achievement. What has often happened is that the full development of everyone is neglected in favor of a highly selective merit system based on academic achievement. From early childhood merit becomes defined as the ability to learn as quickly as other children do—an attitude that is perpetuated when a child enters school.

For some children, this attitude has spelled years of torment and waste. They are the Marginally Learning Disabled (MLD) children, an estimated 10 to 15 percent of the population with IQs between approximately 75 and 95. Some have called them "the shadow children." Too intelligent to be considered retarded yet unable to keep up with their peers in the conventional school setting, they fall between the rungs of the educational ladder. The only thing these so-called slow learners learn fast is failure. Often they are considered so academically hopeless that they not only are excluded from higher education, but most often drop or are thrown out of secondary schools after they have been prodded through inadequate elementary school programs.

No other group of children suffers more in self-esteem or feels more frustrated. Parents are desperate when their children cannot make the grade in school. Many teachers don't understand their special problems and find their presence disruptive of normal classwork. Peers may dislike them for their differences and immaturity. At the end of their formal education, these neglected and unhappy young people may face a future of menial, dead-end jobs—a loss which is so tragically theirs but which also belongs to all of us.

In the past, all too often the helplessness of parents and teachers before the massive problems of the MLD child was compounded by widespread professional ignorance regarding these children. One researcher found thirty-eight labels for this group in the professional literature, although few of the authors attempted to define the terms or conditions under discussion. These children have erroneously been called "lazy" or "late bloomers," labels that have served only to isolate them further. Because of such misunderstanding and confusion, parents have been forced to run from specialist to specialist— neurologists, psychologists, psychiatrists, educational therapists, and optometrists.

In the last decade or so this tragic picture has begun to brighten. There has been some growth in understanding the particular etiology and development of marginal learning disabilities. And even more importantly, educators have begun to realize that learning is for everyone, not just for the traditional student.

This fine and sensitively written book signifies a milestone in this development. It will be of interest and real practical help not only to parents and educators of MLD children, but also to anyone interested in how all human beings learn and grow.

No person perhaps is better able to write about the MLD child than Dr. Judith Ehre Kranes. Once labeled a slow learner herself, she graduated near the bottom of her high-school class. Yet, remarkably she went on to become a specialist in child development and a professor of education.

Thirteen years ago Dr. Kranes founded the Para-Educator Center at New York University, a two-year program that trains people with learning disabilities to be teacher aides in nursery schools, day-care centers, kindergartens, and other helping professions. The brilliance of the program lies in Dr. Kranes's concept that students can learn what they themselves have missed by watching and helping young children in the nursery schools. The program over the years has grown from two students to forty-five, developing from an experiment in Dr. Kranes's home during her off-hours to a Demonstration Center just off Washington Square Park in Manhattan. The center has become a model for similar efforts across the country.

Fortunately, we realize today that many kinds of learning are valuable, not simply academic or technical skills. Educators should prize and help to develop empathy, caring, patience, and sensitivity, as well as cognitive skills. For our society, in truth, depends upon many kinds of merit. No child must be lost to us; we must find for each a place.

John C. Sawhill
President, New York University

PREFACE

New York University's Para-Educator Center for Young Adults, known as PEC for short, educates and trains Marginally Learning Disabled (MLD) young adults, ages approximately eighteen to twenty-two years old, IQs about 75 to 95, to be teacher aides to young children and to work in other helping professions. Although the MLD's academic ability is usually around the fifth-grade level, when applying for admission, these young people most often look and sound like any regular high-school graduate. Yet more often than not, their lives are full of rejection and failure; and just as often, they are isolated and lost.

Because PEC is essentially a Demonstration Center, the enrollment is limited to forty-five students yearly, thereby allowing only a tiny number of the "learning disabled" to attend. On the surface, then, it might appear gratuitous to write a book about this population, the context of which, to a large extent, derives from PEC's work; and, indeed, over the years, for that reason, despite urging to the contrary, I hesitated. But the larger view that has come with time has convinced me that the results of the PEC Program have much of value to offer anyone—but primarily the parents of this population—interested in helping children or young adults with serious learning problems. In fact, there are many implications for those working with children, generally. For one thing, there is almost nothing in the literature at present which concerns itself specifically with MLD young adults, although from the statistics cited by various authorities, PEC's population may represent as much as 10 to 20 percent of the school population—a population that has been woefully neglected in the schools, as well as in research. Further, by the age of eighteen (when the MLD apply to PEC), there is practically no place for them to go except into menial jobs, or those requiring the simplest mechanical and manipulative skills.

For another thing, within the MLD's functioning, they show a considerable potential beside their limitations; but tragically, the abilities they do possess have been overlooked, either in ignorance, or through inadequate educational processes. Thus we find ourselves teaching the PEC young adults about things that they were undoubtedly able to cope with as young children. Parents, and others, will find that much of the material within the PEC design, as presented here, can be used for MLD children, from early childhood onward.

The PEC Program was conceived in 1966 while I was a professor at New York University, but it germinated during the many years before in which I taught children in the regular public and private schools. Indeed, it is those early experiences that led to the child development approach indigenous to the PEC design, and it is the study of the child that has led our MLD young adults to an understanding of the same concepts to which nursery school children are exposed. The MLD young adults learn the kinds of things that most of them missed in their early years, while laying a foundation for later skills; at the same time, they are learning about the child's development on the way to becoming aides in the helping professions. (In effect, it is a play within a play.) In addition, those of us who work with this population have come to realize that *all* MLD young adults benefit from this training, no matter what line of work they undertake after graduation.

The PEC Program is rich in its provisions: it is the only known facility, within a university setting, that has a carefully planned, well-structured, two-year program for the educational and professional development of this young adult population. The processes through which it approaches the cognitive (mental) and creative aspects of their development, along with the professional training, is completely original. In addition, the small size of PEC's population is itself a plus, allowing not only for a rare uniformity, but also for a rare specificity, in the study of this population.

Facing and helping the MLD can be an extraordinarily challenging task. Occasionally, in weariness, and in our zeal to be optimistic and supportive, one may embrace a kind of wishful thinking that covers up reality; but, in the end, if the reality—though it is incredibly painful at times—is made favorable, the entire experience can be fruitful and productive. Hopeless dreams can only lead to a defeat for all involved. In my own efforts, my courage, hope, and strength are constantly restored as I realize that the MLD's wounds *can* be healed, even while the causes and their cure are not known. Happiness is always a by-product. It emerges for our MLD population as they feel PEC's community of acceptance and support; as they, and we, face their deficits honestly and build on their strengths; and as they work very hard to meet PEC's standards, thereby succeeding in a field for which they have talent. This self-fulfillment is the kind of reality that produces its own optimism, as well as genuine achievement.

J.E.K.

1

Guidelines to the Marginally Learning Disabled (MLD)

THE LOST MLD

Mr. and Mrs. Jed Hubeir, from a small town in Tennessee, sat across from me in the PEC Admissions Office. They were a pleasant, attractive couple, probably in their mid-fifties. Their tale matched a countless number of others that parents told us.

"There was nothing wrong with Cary when he was a baby," Mrs. Hubeir said. "In fact, until he was in the second grade no one saw anything wrong."

"What happened in the second grade?"

"Well, he couldn't do the three Rs, and the children shut him out."

"How old was he then?"

"Eight," Mr. Hubeir broke in. "Now you know, Marj," looking at his wife, "there were things that bothered *us* before then." He shook his head, looking at me. "Cary

23

had trouble from kindergarten on. He couldn't crayon between the lines. We were puzzled by him in the way you are puzzled when you're looking at somebody who really *isn't* the somebody you think he is. Whatever he said sounded all right, but when you tried to pursue it, it went up in smoke. Marjorie and I talked about it till we were blue in the face."

"I'm not sure I follow you."

"Well, Cary looked OK as a baby, just as he does now, and he sounded all right, but sometimes he would just seem to switch off; or maybe his switches got confused."

"Wasn't he ever at loose ends the way so many of these children are when they are young? Hyperactive? Perseverative?"

Mrs. Hubeir began, then hesitated. "Well, no. Well, not really, although we didn't know about that kind of behavior until we met some other parents later. Cary was just the opposite; very quiet and passive, really. Wouldn't you agree, Jed? So, when he walked and talked a little later than both of his brothers, we thought it was part of his personality."

"That's right," her husband agreed. "But remember that he had trouble in the first grade." Mr. Hubeir was thoughtful. "The teacher told us that some kids get started later."

"I guess that's when we really got concerned," his wife put in.

Mr. Hubeir scowled. "Miss Perkins, the second-grade teacher, didn't make any bones about it, though. She said something was wrong, only her something was a shocker. She said that Cary had serious emotional problems."

"You didn't agree?"

Mr. Hubeir, reaching for his wallet, pulled out several snapshots. "Here are our older boys," he said, handing me the photos. "Bob's four years older than Cary, Fred two and a half. They're as normal as apple pie. Why should Cary be disturbed?"

I gave some classical reasons. "Well there are the two older boys, and you know about sibling rivalry? And parents can be different with each child."

This time Mrs. Hubeir frowned. "Yes. We've heard all about that, and not the easy way either. My husband and I had to drive to Nashville once a week for therapy together. Then I had to drive Cary in once a week, too," she added. "We didn't spare time or money, and we don't have too much of either. But nothing changed. We finally felt that the doctor was a nitpicker. Thank God for Jed's brother."

Mr. Hubeir agreed. "Tom is on a newspaper. He's always trying to be helpful, and when he sent us the piece about slow learners and the minimally brain damaged, it was an eye-opener. That article got us to a psychologist who put us on the right track. Just the same nothing showed up. Our pediatrician couldn't recall anything that had to do with a birth trauma, and none of us could remember any illness that Cary had that might have injured his brain. The EEG was normal, too. It was the tests that the psychologist gave him that put him in the 'slow learner' category—between the retarded and the normal; what you call the 'marginal.' "

Mrs. Hubeir sighed. "It was then that we sent him off to a school for exceptional children. But I don't know that it was any better than the public school we took him out of."

"Now, Marj." Mr. Hubeir sounded a bit impatient. "They did teach him some reading and writing and number work there."

"Yes," she agreed, "but what he got out of the older grades we'll never know."

"Didn't he make friends?" I asked.

Mrs. Hubeir was not enthusiastic. "Well, at least he

wasn't shut out the way he was in the public school. But then they had so many misfits in that place, with such a wide range of problems that . . ."

Mr. Hubeir interrupted. "You know that he was much happier there, Marjorie. They had a lot of good activities and socials."

"When he came home he would baby-sit for the neighbors." Mrs. Hubeir sounded more cheerful now. "He started with my niece's three-year-old. He's good with children."

"So he told me before in the interview. He is a promising candidate."

The parents were obviously pleased. "When my brother sent the *Saturday Review** article about PEC," Mr. Hubeir said, "we got excited. We both said, 'This is for Cary.' "

"There really isn't anything else," his wife continued, "except some manual training, and most of that is geared for the much more handicapped."

"You tried a workshop?"

"I looked at one in the city," Mr. Hubeir replied. "There was a wide mixture of trainees. Some were terribly disabled. Some looked like boys, some like men in their fifties. We're *not* snobs, but why shouldn't there be the same suitable possibilities for this marginal population as there are for those who don't have learning disabilities? Cary happens to be much better with children than he is with a hammer and a screwdriver."

"You can't imagine the time my husband spent on Cary's problem, Dr. Kranes. He deserves a medal."

"It has been an agonizing search," Mr. Hubeir observed. "Small communities like ours don't know much, and there's nothing in the library about teenagers or young adults like Cary, either."

---

* This article appeared in the *Saturday Review*, October 14, 1972.

Mr. Hubeir must be a good teacher, I thought. Aloud I said, "A lot has been written about the younger learning disabled, especially the retarded."

"It's hard to tell who's who," he replied. "Besides, most of the articles and books I've seen for the younger grades are about physical exercises, or games and gimmicks."

"There's an explosion about the learning disabled now. Things will improve."

"Hopefully, yes," was his response. "Anyway, you've probably heard stories like ours from other parents. What you can't hear is our frustration, the pain it adds up to. It isn't fair that kids like our Cary should be so lost."

Lost they are, I thought to myself, with all of the ferment at present about the "learning disabled." The very looseness of the term itself loses them. How can desperate parents and caring teachers and counselors of what I designate as the Marginally Learning Disabled (MLD) possibly find their children in the written accounts of individuals who appear to be like a Cary Hubeir, but nevertheless who are "succeeding" in the regular secondary or university settings? Is such success possible for those who need years in a special school or special classes, when supporting evidence is so contradictory? Who exactly are the MLD? Where, within the broad framework of the learning disabled, do they belong?

After a weary search in the libraries, among the books about the "neurologically impaired," "mental subordination," "minimally brain damaged," "slow learners," and so on, one finds bits and fragments that fit the profile of a Cary Hubeir; yet, what is usually described as able by some of the professionals, stands far below the MLD's potential, whereas other of their accounts create a star-studded future that makes any MLD success story that I know about look drab. As for MLD young *adults*, like those attending PEC, who are over eighteen, with IQs about 75 to 95, there is practically nothing to be found.

Parents and their children, who apply to PEC, and who have lived through eighteen or more years of frustration, are often desperate. The following quotations fictionalized from PEC admissions and interview records reflect those feelings:

A parent: "The tragedy is that he's so near normal, but no one accepts him anyway. He knows something terrible is wrong, but he doesn't know what, and neither do we. If he really was retarded, he'd be a thousand times better off. We've been looking for something like your program for so long that it's hard to believe it's for real. L. loves children. He's a wonderful baby-sitter."

A school counselor: "She can hardly read or write but she's beautiful when she helps out in our kindergarten with the children. She's disadvantaged and probably brain damaged. She would fit into your program."

A parent: "It's heartbreaking for her and for us. She's not backward enough to belong with the retarded, but she's not good enough to manage in a regular class, either. There just isn't any place to turn to. She loves children. You should see her with her sister's baby."

A parent: "My husband and I have gone from expert to expert since he was four. As a child he couldn't be quiet. They can't tell us anything except maybe he's brain damaged. But the electroencephalogram at New York's Cornell Medical Center didn't show anything wrong, and he looks so normal. He is compassionate with children. Do you think PEC can help him? He likes to work with children."

Office of Vocational Rehabilitation (OVR) counselor: "We have nothing for her in our state programs. She is so borderline that it would not be healthy to put her in the programs we have to offer. They're full of the extremely retarded and the extremely handicapped. Your program sounds right for her."

A *parent:* "The schools have always told us J. can't learn. Some of them say she is minimally retarded. We put her in the workshops but they were completely inappropriate. We couldn't believe it when we heard about PEC. She's very good with children. Trouble is she hasn't any friends of her own age."

A *parent:* "Yes, she's pretty and she looks normal enough. They had her working in the back room, couldn't understand why she didn't want to work in the office. Finally they pushed her out front. Well, she got all of the messages mixed up, and she was afraid of just that. She really loves children but until we heard about this program we didn't know she could be trained to work with them."

A *school counselor:* "The schools haven't been able to fit him anywhere, but he was good at a camp for exceptional children. I think your program would be right for him."

A *parent:* "We have never found a school where he could learn much. He does like children. Maybe he would fit here."

The students' view of themselves is equally poignant:

"My parents really wish I was dead. They think I don't know, but they really can't stand me being special. Yes, I like working with children. I worked at a camp for exceptional children and I'm good at it. I'm not good at reading though."

"I hated school. I have learning problems, but I can love children."

"Do your students look different? I want to be a teacher aide, but I don't want to be with students that look different."

"I'd like to get a diploma. I'd like some friends, too. Could I make friends in the PEC Program?"

"No, I'm not good at math or reading. I'm a good baby-sitter. I'd like to be a teacher aide."

Unfortunately, most educators are as confused as the Marginally Learning Disabled themselves, and their parents. In meetings with professional groups, who are interested in hearing about PEC's work, invariably those who work with the retarded (under about 70 IQ) view the MLD as "normal," and able to function independently, whereas those who teach the normal (about 100 IQ and above) view them as "retarded." The following taped comments typify the confusions. They were recorded during the question-and-answer period, at a conference for professionals, after PEC's work had been presented through slides and the students' papers:

"Why do you bother with these students? *They* have no problems. If you work with the retarded, you'll find out what problems are."

"How do you dare place these students with normal children [in fieldwork placements]? It's just got to have a bad effect on normal youngsters growing up. What do the parents of the nursery say?" (As will be seen later, most of the children's parents are very sympathetic; some have, or know other parents who have, a child like our PEC students.)

"Did your students really do that homework? It's hard to believe that a population like that can have that much understanding."

"No wonder your PEC is having so much success. You're really working with normal students, even if you don't know it."

Occasionally we have come upon a few people in the audience who have worked with these in-between students, although at much younger ages than ours at PEC. One summarized their responses when she said, "It just shows what can happen when these unfortunate students get into a program that understands and knows what to do with them."

Obviously, the Marginally Learning Disabled need some careful identification if they are to be rescued from oblivion.

APPROPRIATE IDENTIFICATION

Genius! Normal! Dull! Borderline! Brain damaged! Moron! Imbecile! The words leap out at us—words created by man out of dreamed-up scratchings, meant as innocent tools for communication and understanding. But, like the shape of a beautiful woman, or a knife, what pleasure, terror, anger, or even poison these images evoke in our minds, especially once they become labels. The loose terminology of "learning disabled" was undoubtedly intended to relieve the problem, but, unfortunately, it compounds the difficulty, including, as it does, an individual with learning difficulties at any level be he bright, average, dull, or retarded.*

New labels, of course, can mean a fresh and profitable approach, and it is about time to free the child from the tags that imprison him. In addition, with the increased understanding of the many factors that constitute mental functioning—factors such as physical ability, emotional stability, and social experience—the broadened view of intelligence renders the old labels obsolete. As in many reform movements from which the term "learning disabled" emerged, important issues were increasingly obscured, with no group suffering more than the group that

---

* To avoid awkward phrasing, the generic pronouns "he," "his" and "him" are used to designate both male and female.

has *never* been clearly defined; that is, individuals known variously as "dull," "subnormal," "slow learner," "minimally brain damaged," "exceptional," and by an endless number of other labels. Under the heading of "learning disabilities," this population is more lost than ever.

The MLD are the in-between group—not retarded, and yet not quite normal. Anyone learning new concepts, be he child or adult, able or disabled, realizes how much easier it is to grasp the extreme ends of an idea. Often, to make something clearer, we talk in extremes: "genius-retarded," "tall-short," "black-white," "top-bottom," instead of the gradations that fall between those poles; coping with matters that are "relative to" requires some kind of distinguishing marks, or handles.

The first handle in coping with an idea is an appropriate designation, through a name or a label, that marks its unusual qualities. In order to distinguish this population from others in the learning disabled category, the crux and focus of the label must bear upon a certain unity of features particular to it. The qualities common to the population under consideration here are an overall IQ measurement of approximately 75 to 95, with the *basic* problem being one of a disability in learning, usually of a subtle nature, and not of emotional maladjustment. These people, judging by academic results, have—despite no overt hearing or sight impairment—perceptual problems that appear to reflect a skewing of what they see and hear. As young children, they may or may not have been hyperactive and perseverative. With appropriate pedagogical methods, their learning does improve; and as young adults, they can function with wisdom and judgment. The learning disabilities are 'thought to be neurological in origin. Within the approximate 75 to 95 IQ borders, these common traits identify the Marginally Learning Disabled. This group, however, like all others, has many types and degrees within their particular learning disability range.

INTELLIGENCE

Intelligence is a slippery customer. My own questions began consciously to be formulated after I left the public grades to teach in the private "progressive" schools. In that atmosphere, there was much more time in the schedule for children to show themselves (in the early history of progressive education there was too much time), and fortunately, there were many different kinds of opportunities through which the teacher could see the child apply himself.

I found myself asking: Is the high achiever, who has a fine ability to manipulate verbal, written, and number symbols, more intelligent than the omnivorous reader who could write a beautiful composition on Abraham Lincoln, say, but who could not handle math and science? Or how about the eleven-year-old who could read only with the greatest difficulty, but who could look at a doorknob that did not work, take it off, and in a matter of minutes have it back in good working order? Then there were the students who appeared mediocre in intellectual areas, but who were resourceful and dynamic in creative work that demanded the use of skills different from the verbal and written ones.

In addition, what of children like the MLD, who, in school, suffer when the cognitive is necessary to solve the more abstract problems, but who are sensitive to and shrewd about problem solving in practical and human situations? The philosopher Susanne Langer says of intelligence that "if one door is closed to it, it finds or even breaks another entrance to the world." Hopefully, yes. But in my estimation, intelligence, defined by many teachers and clinicians as innate capacity or potentiality, can ride underground forever, if the environment does not nourish and stimulate it; and the environment must also provide some doors for its release.

At best, very few individuals use their full capacity; nor do I believe that the ceiling of intelligence is the same for all people, just as none of us has equal ability in physical skills, science, or in the field of art. But never knowing how high the ceiling is, good teachers always seek to lengthen their students' reach; their success is constantly illuminated in the stimulating and resourceful classroom, be the students learning or non-learning disabled. In fact, the good methods used in the regular classrooms of earlier years are excitingly effective with MLD individuals—which, I may say, is what primarily brought me into their world. Many examples of those earlier experiences, in what was then known as the ungraded classroom, and which I much later used in working with the MLD, come to my mind.

Nita, a student I taught many years ago, was eleven years old and the slowest child in her class. She was the youngest of three siblings, the other two of whom were dropouts from school, one in a job as a truck driver, and one working in a shoe factory with her father. Sour, ill-tempered, and touchy, Nita constantly picked fights with her peers. She was uninterested and inattentive in all her academic subjects and her achievement tests showed her to be on the third-grade level.

I watched Nita carefully, trying to divert and redirect her as she horsed around. One day, in sewing class, she jokingly fixed a large piece of material around her black hair, but cleverly and with style. That led to my persuading her to search through a bag of remnants with me so that she could make a bandanna hat for herself.

Nita's fingers grew clever as she grew interested, and without any of her usual resistance, she went shopping with the student teacher for needles, thread, binding, and other necessary material. This also led to her shopping after school for personal things with me—but that came much later. Cumbersomely and slowly, she learned to add and subtract in double columns, and to do simple multiplication and division, as she had to make change; she also learned to use a tape measure, when her finished hat gave way to napkins that she made for her mother's birthday, and to handkerchiefs she sewed for her family as Christmas presents.

Nita's reading progressed, too, as we wrote simple sewing directions on cards for her; these she had to read before we would help her, though we sometimes broke the rule at the beginning out of exasperation. Sewing became the motivating force in Nita's life, and although she remained short-tempered, she became more pleasant as she settled down. When she left the junior high school, no one was surprised that it was to take a job in the local sewing factory.

Nita's overall IQ was given to me as 80. That score guided the school in her grade placement, but I have no doubt that had she been tested before she quit school, her score would have stretched substantially—maybe by ten points. Whether her learning disability in school was due to her culture, or to some inherent physical dysfunction, will never be known. In those days we didn't know enough to ask; we were simply delighted that her "reach" was substantially lengthened.

Another student also comes to my mind, when I think of the short reach. Hans was ten years old, with an overall IQ of 85. His father was an apartment-house superintendent, and his one sister, age eighteen, was a housekeeper for a neighbor. Generally, Hans was ineffectual, timid, and noticeably lacking in self-confidence. He could manage third-grade arithmetic, but he had great trouble with any subject that involved reading skills. The only interests Hans showed were in trading baseball cards, and in the game itself, although his physical skills were not very good.

Discussion about Hans with the physical education teacher, Mr. Burns, led him to take the boy on as a kind of assistant referee and sports manager; off the field, for the two ungraded classes, Hans would get the equipment in order, distribute notices, and so on. We also created a sports section for the front bulletin board; Hans was put in charge of it, with the help of another classmate, Jerry, who, although much better in reading than Hans, was epileptic, with a deaf ear as well. The two boys had to follow the rules that no news item could be put on the bulletin board without an appropriate heading, written by them. Imagine our surprise, then, when Hans asked Miss Abard, the student teacher, whether their coverage could go beyond school affairs, including the major and minor league activities, with personal interest stories about Babe Ruth, and other great sports figures.

Hans spent a full half hour every day working on phonetic cards Miss Abard would make out of the problems connected with his baseball activities. I can still remember Hans walking around the class, repeating the questions I sometimes put to him that tickled his fancy: "When is a fowl not a foul?" and "Is an umpire ever an empire?"

Meanwhile Hans gradually moved from the unnoticed "here" in the attendance book, to one whose companionship became actively sought by his peers; and on open-school night, when his parents timidly showed up, scrubbed and polished, they brought a huge cake for the class that Hans's mother had baked, as an expression of appreciation for Hans's transformation. We were sad to lose Hans the next year, when the family moved to Canada, where a relative got his father a better job; but we know that Hans left us with a substantially longer reach.

THE IQ TEST

Does the definition of intelligence as innate capacity or potentiality render the IQ obsolete? Until some test comes along that does measure intrinsic ability, the IQ performs a valuable service, despite its being sloughed aside by many of today's educators, who not only are torn by politics, but who are preoccupied with the subject of equality in the schools. But within the struggle the differences among the students loom sharper than ever, and teachers are finding it increasingly difficult to manage them. For this reason, now more than ever, the IQ test is necessary.

We know intelligence only by what it enables us to do; it is not a tangible reality. The IQ test is a tool that measures academic skills and the knowledge the child has gained—the purpose for which the measurement was originally intended. It also predicts scholastic performance, and in the hands of the informed educator, who knows only too well *the weakness of a single score*, it serves as a valuable guide. Nevertheless, to many people concerned about equality, it constitutes an unqualified menace; reference to it in the literature for the layman is studiously avoided. Such denial seems at cross-purposes, especially in the learning disabled field, because before the existence of the intelligence test, it was impossible to define or diagnose those who were learning disabled.

The IQ test has also been maligned for not being fair to all cultures. While there has been some effort to control the socio-cultural bias, none of the recent tests have been much more successful in that regard.

CHRONOLOGICAL AGE

One can never be sure what exactly is meant by the "child," known these days as the "kid," partly because age levels which constitute an important boundary line have also become unpopular. Unpopular or not, as the remarkable psychologist Jean Piaget and his followers have demonstrated, children display a similarity in comprehension, within a certain chronological framework, in their stages of thinking. In our culture, for example, before kindergarten age, unless deliberately taught, the child does not know his last name; nor, at age four, does he understand that a mother and a wife are the same person; nor that a storekeeper is the husband and not the father of his nursery school teacher. Even bright eight-year-olds are surprised to learn that their regular teacher is also a student. "*You* go to school!" they exclaim. Without some boundary lines of age, teachers are frequently left at sea, as evidenced by the disorder and chaos often rampant in the open classroom.

A basic standard for the judgment of a child's performance includes a knowledge of his chronological age. The first question of the seasoned educator, when told the child is "bright," or "dull," is to ask how old he is; without chronological age, such terminology is not meaningful. Dr. Arnold Gesell, a pioneer in the field of child development, was able to evolve what proved to be an invaluable frame of reference based on maturity profiles and stages of growth; his studies revealed that in the process of development, each child is born not only with a potential that is uniquely his, but, also, that there are basic trends and growth sequences which are typical for all children. It is, of course, the similarities within the chronological framework that provide a basic homogeneity for the teacher's approach; but at the same time his methods must account for the unique differences.

Even the best categorizations by age, label, and IQ can be open to reproach, especially for a population like PECs, whose problems are complex and multiply determined. Disabled or not, individual abilities are not easily confined; and for that reason alone, the lines must be drawn if educators are to recognize those whom they wish to help, and communicate about them effectively. With the most fitting of categorizations, there is mystery enough to grapple with.

BEYOND A LABEL, AGE, OR IQ

At his healthiest, the individual's search for his identity is ongoing; at the same time, in seeking guidelines to the identity of those others whom we wish to help, be they offspring, pupils, or patients, we know that the pegs of a label, age, or IQ are only the crudest openings to such an understanding.

The MLD population usually looks and sounds normal; and as they adopt ways that help them feel closer to their society, they may add to the perplexity of those who try to understand their handicap. This was true of a very attractive girl named Sema, who would carry books under her arm wherever she went, the titles carefully showing, but which she had the greatest difficulty read-

ing or understanding, and in which she had little interest. At the same time, individuals like Sema may have a
great facility in holding on to and repeating what they
hear from others—an enviable skill, much like the very
young child who learns the words of a story after hearing
it twice, and knows it better than the reader.

But the MLD individual *can* and *does* apply what he
hears, if the message is not too complicated, and if it
deals with a social situation, and particularly with his
personal self. Also, it is a great mistake to claim, as many
do, that this population, and the retarded, cannot abstract. Anyone who can interpret pictures, use or read
words and/or numbers in communicating in however
primitive a fashion, is extracting the meaning out of symbols—is abstracting to some degree; but the further away
the word is from the real thing—the more removed the
symbol is from the thing it stands for—the quicker the
MLD gets lost. For example, they can readily connect
the picture of an apple—or the word—with an apple, if
they have seen or eaten one. But the term "fruit" is a bit
harder for them to comprehend and "fruit" as "produce"
is even more difficult.

Prolonged listening to, or conversing with, most MLD
may finally reveal some of their difficulties in comprehension. This discussion took place with ten-year-old
Harry, IQ 78, in a school for exceptional children.

"My teacher got mad at me today."

"You must have done something to upset the group."

"All I did was to talk to Jason."

"When was that?"

"Social studies."

"Was Mrs. Bales teaching?"

"Yes."

"Didn't that make it difficult for you and Jason to hear
her?"

"Yeah."

"Didn't it disturb the others?"

"I don't know. Maybe."

"Didn't it make it harder for Mrs. Bales to teach?"

"I don't see why."

"When you are talking to a friend and another friend is talking to him at the same time, don't you find that hard?"

"Two of us wouldn't talk to him at the same time."

"But three of you were talking at the same time: you and Jason and the teacher."

"That's a different thing."

"Why is it different? How?"

"Just Jason and me were talking; that's not three."

"But Mrs. Bales was talking, too, and that makes three."

"Well, she wasn't talking *just* to Jason."

"She was talking to *everyone*, and that meant Jason and you. Neither of you listened."

"Yeah, I knew why she was mad."

And there is no doubt that Harry *did* understand why his teacher was "mad" despite his confusion about the analogy of the "two" in his mind, with the "three" who were talking. Like the younger child, his understanding is being influenced by what *he* sees and experiences, thus he is unable to generalize or operate on theory—to realize that an idea or thing may stay the same even though the obvious conditions can change. I have taught fifth graders who judge a pound of soap powder in a large box to be more than a pound held in a smaller size. The reader may well realize that the advertising market often succeeds even in deceiving the nonhandicapped thinking consumer on this basis; wishful thinking often overtakes intelligence.

An example of some young adults' perplexities in abstracting during a PEC Child Study class discussion reveals their difficulty in comprehension, when the question or statement is couched in words that are far removed from the action. Here the class was reading and discussing the child's social development, while getting ready for the following week's homework. It proceeded easily enough until I posed the thought-provoking adage at the end. This time I asked, "Why is it important for a teacher to practice what he preaches?"

A number of students raised their hands and said that they did not understand the question. I then asked, "What does 'practice' mean?"

"Practice the piano."

"Practice the guitar."

"So?"

"Doing it over and over again."

"Can you sometimes play without the sheet music?"

"Memorizing!"

"Learning by heart!"

"OK, good. Practice is to do it over and over again; learn it by heart." But the class still looked puzzled.

"What does 'preach' mean?"

One boy calls out, "Preach a sermon in church."

"What's a sermon?" Some turn to their junior dictionaries, which they need that day for their tutoring sessions, and they begin to look it up. They give various meanings. Then one alights on "lecture."

"Lecture is best," I say. "Who else gives a lecture besides the minister or rabbi?"

"My mother!"

"You!"

"The state patroller!"

"Great. Practice the way you preach."

A young lady's hand then shot up. Triumphantly she said, "Do what you tell others to do."

Upon that, a number of students eagerly gave examples of this adage, both from their fieldwork placements, and out of their own personal experiences.

Jane said, "A lot of my teachers would tell us to be nice to each other, but they weren't always so nice."

"My older sister says I should always tell the truth, then she tells me to answer the phone and tell some boyfriend she's not home," came from George.

The next year I revised the question to, "Why is it important for a teacher to behave the way he wants his children to behave?" Most of the students could deal easily with the question when it was put that way.

Often as I watch one of these fine, attractive young adults grappling with their problems in comprehension, his image begins to shimmer, as if I were seeing him in a clean, moving stream of water, or in a slightly convex mirror, where the image gets slightly distorted. One cannot examine the mental process itself, but it is clear that, in abstract reasoning, when left on their own resources, many MLD cannot weave together the necessary parts between the proposal or question to the answer—that is, to the logical outcome; at the same time, they may take the steps with help, but at the end the difficulty in integrating the idea results in a lack of comprehension, as if there were a breakdown in their mental circuit.

Too often, these difficulties meet with an adult's impatience and censure, thus increasing the MLD's sense of inadequacy, and rendering him still more impotent. Fortunately, as we have seen in the PEC Program, with the right kind of help and encouragement, the MLD can become productive adults, who can take their place in the world.

ETIOLOGY

Among professionals, "minimal brain damage" is a common label for the MLD. In most cases, despite little or no manifestation of any neuromotor dysfunction, this population is usually considered neurologically impaired, with an overgrowth of psychological problems as a result of the impairment. The disorders in the learning behavior that may be apparent appear to be the result of perceptual difficulties and difficulties in integrating ideas. Whatever the etiology, the learning disorders are much more subtle than those that usually fit the classical brain-damage syndrome.

The assault to the child's organism may occur either in the genetic development of the child, the prenatal, perinatal, or postnatal period, or during birth. Among the causes for the damage may be genetic malformations, some external trauma, lack of oxygen, or an infectious disease. The MLD's difficulties may not be apparent immediately, for many parts of the brain do not function at birth; moreover, learning that is embedded in the whole array of communication skills, and social and cognitive processing, develop gradually, as well as being in demand later in the child's existence. Some authorities believe that the nature of the child's learning problems changes as he grows older because of the increased maturity within his biological development.

Be that as it may, Dr. Herbert Birch, who, until his recent death, was a professor at the Albert Einstein College of Medicine, considered the term "brain damage," minimal or otherwise, unfortunate, for it implies the existence of knowledge about causes where none exist, as well as leading to a stereotyped view of the label itself. At the same time, he indicated that children with problems under the label, who do not show evidence of neurological damage, do constitute an important clinical group.

Presently, the diagnosis of brain damage in the young child may be partially tied up with disordered behavior, short attention span, defective work habits, impulsiveness, and specific learning disorders. The problems in learning include reading below grade level, a gap between oral skill and comprehension, and a general inability to cope with abstractions, among other things.

Some of our PEC parents report that, as children, our young adults displayed many of the frenetic characteristics commonly described in the picture of the brain damaged. But the hyperactivity, distractibility, and impulsivity are rarely apparent by the time that we see them at the age of eighteen, or older, possibly because—as the neurologist Dr. Leon Eisenberg and other authorities hold—by late childhood, the hyperactive syndromes are likely to diminish, and by adolescence are either hardly noticeable or disappear altogether.

What is common to the majority of all PEC students is their marked difficulties in learning—their reading scores stand at about the fifth-grade level—as well as their marked perceptual problems. These turn up in one or more of their classes: child study, environmental science, music and dance, art, home economics, or shop. Interestingly enough, a student who does not evince perceptual problems in his written work may show them in one or more of his other classes; or contrariwise, his written words and letters may be twisted, with large spaces in between, yet he may perform without any apparent perceptual problems in some of his other classes. Occasionally PEC young adults manifest no difficulties in perception. If there are no other signs of neurological damage in his records either, and when his performance has been successful, we conclude that his learning difficulties are the result of external circumstances.

Put simply, perception, defined as "to know," is the process of discrimination; it leads to thinking, learning, and communicating, and it involves all of man's sensory factors; from these the brain sorts out millions of bits of data. To survive, the individual must constantly perceive: according to Dr. Ray H. Barsch, a professor of Special

Education, he must, "scan, appraise, evaluate, select, and act," with the ability to transmit stimuli to the brain and interpret them accurately.

Perceptual disturbances usually refer to the gross tendency of the performer to perceive in unaccepted ways. These distortions may take place even when, on the surface, a child's sensory organs function very well, for the stimuli of one or more of them may be modified as they move along the nerve fibers to the brain; or the brain itself may misinterpret or not recognize the messages, thus making for confusion. Distortions such as skewed figures, spatial disorganization, the inability to discriminate between background and foreground, between different kinds of sound, or, tactically, between different fabrics may be some of the consequences. Still, there is no doubt that the MLD perceive many things accurately, just as the nonhandicapped learner occasionally misperceives.

According to Dr. Willard Abraham and Dr. Christine P. Ingram, about 15 to 20 percent of all schoolchildren stand within the PEC IQ range of approximately 75 to 95; most have extreme perceptual problems. The more recent research of Rosa Hagin and Dr. Achie Silver, of the New York University Medical School, covering a much wider population, places one-third of any kindergarten class as likely to be vulnerable to learning problems and concomitant underachievement. Unquestionably, many of Hagin and Silver's population have learning disabilities that are exogenous—external to the organism—in origin. But a number suffer from perceptual disorders, many of whom appear to belong to the PEC population. Dr. William Cruickshank, and other psychologists who have a neurological orientation, believe that when the cause of a child's learning problems is not exogenous, the disabilities *always* have a neurological basis. Dr. Cruickshank believes that the tremendous problems of this population are being over-looked because too few psychologists and educators have training in the basic sciences. He contends that most parents (who find it easier not to face the complex neurophysiological aspects of the problem) need a more knowledgeable leadership from professionals.

MAINSTREAMING

In education, mainstreaming is a commonly used term. It describes the movement of breaking down segregation practices by integrating minority and special groups into classrooms that contain the overall majority population. In the push to broaden the base by including the learning handicapped, the passage of the Education for All Children Act, Public Law 94-142, which became effective October 1, 1977, turned the drive into an established practice.

There has already been an enormous amount of publicity given to this highly involved and complicated law, accompanied by much controversy. From Drs. Seymour Sarason and John Doris's abbreviated version of it, implementation of 94-142 requires that handicapped and nonhandicapped must be taught together, in public and private schools, to the extent possible. September 1978 proclaimed the time when all handicapped children, ages three to eighteen, must have a public education that is free and suitable, and by September 1980 this will be true for all handicapped ages three to twenty-one; an appropriate education must be provided for the handicapped who have been receiving an inadequate education, or who were receiving none at all.

Among the issues covered by the law are those dealing

with nondiscriminatory tests and evaluation, parental participation, and the development of educational plans for each child; these individual plans are to be reviewed yearly by a representative of each school district, and the child's parents and teacher. The administration of this law, the funds involved, and the criteria through which it will be administered, among many other things, are mind-boggling.

The most active majority behind the mainstreaming of the handicapped learner treats it as if it were a political rather than an educational issue, possibly because few of its major proponents are teachers in either the special or regular classrooms. Consequently, teachers who question the wisdom of mainstreaming a large number of the handicapped are often accused of treating them as a different species of human beings, and shutting them out of the broader community.

Because of most MLD's normal appearance, the subtlety of the learning problems, and the present inadequacy of medical diagnoses, no learning disabled group has been more frequently and consistently overlooked in the regular classroom; nor is there any learning disabled population that needs a special classroom setting more than they.

The overall and most obvious school characteristic of the MLD is their consistent inability to keep up with the regular students in academic subjects, remaining, despite any improvement in results, markedly behind their peers of the same age. Usually, in written work, their expression is extremely constrained, in comparison with their verbal output, even among the most able, and it usually reflects a number of perceptual difficulties, which makes it impossible for them to learn adequately with traditional approaches to education. As these students grow older, most of their feelings of inadequacy increase, leading them to drop out of the regular schools. A few may express deviant, antisocial, or some form of unacceptable behavior, for if they are not depressed, they are angered and antagonized by the rejection and belittlement that they experience in the regular school setting.

Many parents of MLD and their children have expressed reactions to this type of placement:

Parent: "It was such torture that we were almost relieved when she got to the third grade and we were told she would have to go into the special class."

Daughter: "I couldn't do the work and I didn't have any friends."

Parent: "They didn't know what to do with her so they just shoved her on."

Daughter: "I felt dumb. I couldn't keep up, but the teachers were nice to me."

Parent: "He never learned anything and the kids made fun of him."

Son: "Yes, I like to read; I'm good at math, too." This boy could not manage a storybook our students must read to four-year-olds; nor could he subtract $3.50 from $5.00, although he gave every indication that he had the ability.

Parent: "The school couldn't figure her out; they kept saying she was emotionally disturbed. But therapy didn't help her either."

Daughter: "I'm tired of being called retarded."

Parent (who insisted in placing her son in the same private school his sister was in): "The school created all kinds of problems for him. They didn't understand him."

Son: "I didn't have any learning problems. I just didn't like the kids." (This applicant had learning problems which, unfortunately, he could acknowledge no better than his parents. He had much better ability than he showed—indeed, he could have succeeded at PEC, but his hostility about his disabilities being projected onto everyone else overshadowed all of his strengths to such a degree that it was impossible for him to succeed.)

The MLD do need to be in a special classroom setting, with sympathetic, resourceful teachers, and remedial specialists, but the special settings presently available are too often inappropriate. Largely this is because budgetary problems force schools to teach the MLD, the very retarded, and the emotionally disturbed, who may be delinquent, together; also, many teachers need better training. The comments of some parents and MLD children reflect this situation:

Parent: "The teacher taught them out of watered-down textbooks, as if they had miniature brains. They need different methods."

Son: "It was OK."

Parent: "First we took him out of the public school and sent him to _____ [a school for exceptional children]. That left a lot to be desired but at least he wasn't looked down on."

Son: "I liked it but a lot of kids were wild and some got into trouble."

Parent: "Is it being high-hat to want your child in a class where the children aren't so extremely retarded— just the opposite of the public school she was in? I don't know which is worse for her."

Daughter: "That class [for exceptional children] made me feel dumber than ever."

In a class with the retarded, the MLD stands out as superior. The markedly retarded, especially those whose handicaps keep them at the lower end of the scale, usually deviate in appearance, and often in speech patterns and behavior; also there is a generalized intellectual inferiority, with a degree of incapacity that most often cannot be overcome, no matter how sound the remedial measures. At the age of fourteen, say, a conspicuously retarded child who is on the second-grade level in reading is likely to be on about that level in all subject matter, whereas an MLD child, if fourth grade in arithmetic, could be third grade in reading, and, at the same time, do well in such classes as music, art, or shop.

Mixing the majority of MLD with the unhandicapped learner, or the retarded, is not only an impossible attempt to do justice to the conglomeration of their learning needs, but it has serious consequences for their emotional development as well. As one might expect, the MLD is most easily tolerated in the regular classroom when there are only one or two, but their experience has shown them where they are not accepted.

One attempt by educators to solve some of the difficulties of mainstreaming is the creation of special classes, outside of the regular classroom, for those with severe learning problems to attend; but relegating the MLD throughout the day to such departmentalization will make for a lack of order and stability to which they adjust very poorly. Essential to their welfare, at any age level, is structure; the majority need both a regular schedule from which they can anticipate and plan, and a routine of activities, with occasional exceptions to allow for some flexibility. For the most part, they also do better under one teacher, with whom they can have a close, supportive relationship.

Teaching techniques, furthermore, should be especially designed, with subject matter sequentially processed to provide stepping-stones for the gaps in comprehension. This is a very different approach from that of the watered-down textbooks most commonly used for the MLD, or from the use of texts meant for the non-learning disabled.

Much has been made of the MLD's need to be in the

regular classroom, on the theory that these individuals will then be able to move from it to the outside world with ease. *It is easy to forget that, until the present time, most MLD are being taught in the regular classroom with contrary results. They remain isolated and lost.* The claim that to place the MLD in classes that are especially designed for their needs is an antidemocratic form of segregation loses sight of the segregation inevitable in the regular setting where teachers can barely cope with the disparities in the homogeneous classroom of the normal-learning population; it also overlooks such students' attitudes, and what is likely to be the teacher's own lack of interest in teaching the handicapped learner.

In a good social adjustment, for the learning or non-learning disabled, it is essential for the child to feel at home with himself. This kind of confidence grows as the adults—be they teachers, parents, or therapists—accept him, with all of his faults, while supporting and helping him in his struggles and successes in learning. Further, he learns best in a school environment that fosters feelings of loyalty, humility, and admiration for those human traits that the child can respect, playing down the hostility generated by the politics of "instant gratification," and "instant equality."

I have spent a long life teaching children of all kinds, of all ages, and in the best and worst schools, public and private, and I have yet to see any child, on his own steam, complain about being in a good classroom, *without some kind of adult influence.* A child takes in feelings of pride, shame, or disgrace, through example. In the end, perhaps it would be more constructive for child and parents if the school could be left in the hands of able educators; and healthier still, if politics, no matter under whose control, were taken out of academic life forever.

2

The MLD
and the
Heart of the Matter

THE RELATIONSHIP OF
EMOTIONAL AND COGNITIVE
DEVELOPMENT

Most parents of children, non-learning or learning disabled, are aware of the many helpful books about the child's emotional need for parental love, acceptance, and support—and they know that meeting such needs is primary to the child's welfare. They are less likely, however, to realize the ways through which they can help in other areas of the child's growth, particularly those that bear on his cognitive or mental expansion. While neither feeling nor thinking develops in isolation, the whole is better nurtured when we are aware of the different components that form it and if we can provide the nutrients for each as it evolves and fuses.

An emotional or feeling response does not represent verifiable fact. A loving child, who may express his momentary anger with his mother with, "I don't like you," is obviously not exhibiting the full score of his emotions; then, too, since feelings are personal and rarely static, they cannot be judged true or false by any objective measure.

Cognition refers to activities in which use of the mind or thinking is prevalent. A cognitive or mental response is provable; to talk or think about a doll, a human being, a hammer, or a tree, denotes objects and their properties; hence objectivity is brought into play. For most individuals, cognition begins as one experiences the concrete object; the child's or adult's first introduction to a hammer usually consists of eyeing and feeling it, and trying it out; very young children may also smell and taste it. At any rate, in one way or another, we use our sensory apparatus for a basic understanding; the child's comprehension, to begin with, is wholly dependent on the use of his sensory organs.

Hearing about a cow may be the youngster's first step in learning about the animal; seeing it in a picture book is another step, although the cow is likely to remain small and brown or white, if it so appeared in the illustration, unless a real cow is brought into view. The cinema can present a truer image than the picture book, of course, but the farmer, who cares for the animal, will know it best of all. Whatever experiences increase the child's knowledge, it becomes clear, in the process of learning, that cognitive development can be endless and very exciting.

Still, parents and teachers can get caught up in an overriding concern for the child's mental growth, or be overly involved with his emotional development, forgetting that both areas need to grow together. In this connection, I am reminded of Mrs. Grole's predicament.

Upon entrance to the PEC Program, Lila Grole's full IQ score was 75, with a verbal of 82 and nonverbal of 69.

By graduation, her full score had moved up to 81, with the verbal 89 and the nonverbal 74. Her personal development was also highly satisfactory, so it did not surprise us when, upon graduation, she was hired to be a teacher aide.

After Lila graduated, Mrs. Grole said, "My oldest daughter, Jackie, is brilliant; all through school she walked away with all of the honors, and everybody admired her intellect. But now that she's got her diploma, all she does is stay home, sleep late, and listen to the stereo. For years we worried about Lila. Now we think she's better off than Jackie, with all of Jackie's brains."

Mrs. Grole's concern took me back to some of my earlier experiences in teaching junior-high students. Many of them grew up to be mature, wholesome adults; occasionally, however, some of the very bright and genius-level students did not fulfill their promise. A few of them, graduating into jobs that demanded intellect of the highest order, remained undeveloped in their life experiences; others, after stumbling around for much of their young adulthood, finally settled into a kind of general mediocrity. I knew most of these intellectually superior students throughout their growing-up years. Now that I look back, they had in common parents and teachers, who, regarding their high mental aptitude as a jeweled crown, treated them with an obeisance that buckled them under their royal headdress.

In response to the years of concentration on the intellect, there arose in the forties, largely with the progressive movement in education, a major emphasis on the child's emotional needs, in what might be regarded as an anti-intellectual operation. At its worst, this was interpreted by the English educator A. S. Neill and his followers as "happiness always means goodness"; or, "Well, that's the basis of school—putting the emotions first, for, you see, nothing of importance comes from the head."

Such catering to the feelings leads to the "psychology of unobstructed need," as writer Irving Howe put it.

Probably in reaction to this overemphasis on the child's emotional needs, with its untidy permissiveness, there sprang up in certain corners of education, in the 1960s, another swing toward the intellect. Largely responsible for these developments were certain technological advances, as well as B. F. Skinner's and other behaviorists' work with animals.

Some of the proponents of the behaviorist approach appear to have shifted from the earlier coddling of the child's emotions to the coddling of the brain. They place a conspicuous emphasis on the youngster's mental development, with an extensive drilling on the acquisition of skills and techniques, producing a child who can handle verbal and number symbols by the age of three and four, and who enters the first grade sounding like a miniature adult. At the same time, this child cannot comprehend the difference between reality and fantasy in a number of situations, having to do with cause and effect. Still, his ability to verbalize, playing back what he has learned, will not reveal this angle of his thinking to those who see the product without understanding the mental process.

With the derision some of these advocates express about earlier educators' concerns for the child's welfare, it may not be surprising that their carefully drilled toddlers often show up in the schools later as children who, although extraordinarily verbal, seem dwarfed as human beings. They relate poorly to people, or to any responsibility for their own acts; neither do they play well, nor demonstrate much feeling or imagination. Indeed one wonders if these behaviorist subjects may not begin to fulfill the fears of Huxley, Orwell, and other writers, in their description of the mechanical man, who has all the skills for responding, but without any self-energizing or self-motivating forces.

Piaget, the twentieth-century giant in the field of child development, repeatedly demonstrates how much the child's mental growth is dependent on the interaction of experience and the child's sensory and motor development. Repeatedly, he highlights the slow and complex process of the youngster's inner development, tying it up with the child's actions, as he examines the period from birth to adolescence. Piaget's extraordinary ingenuity, techniques, and methods can be suggestive to MLD parents and teachers; in his portraits, we see the child, while he flounders in his trial-and-error attempts to grasp the correct idea, living and reliving the activities in which he is involved. He gradually extends his knowledge, as he moves into new and different situations. Above all, as we come to understand the way the child assimilates outward reality, and accommodates to it, we realize that the mechanical response is empty.

THE NEED FOR EXPERIENCE IN PROBLEM SOLVING

Much of the literature in the learning disabled field is devoted to training activities for young children in physical movement, sensory-motor areas, and in ocular and form perception. These have grown out of research about the child's learning difficulties in motor and auditory discrimination, language and speech skills, and in the child's problems in self-perception.

A lot of this matter seems irrelevant to many MLD, because generally their overt physical and motor development appear reasonably good—one reason why their learning handicap too often goes unnoticed. On the other hand, the majority of MLD display difficulties similar to the kind that Professors Doris Johnson and Helmer Myklebust describe in their work with a population that appears to be much more generally and extremely dyslexic, with the academic learning problems far more obvious; at the same time, the subjects of their study are on a higher cognitive level.

As Johnson and Myklebust deal with their individuals' troubles in the three Rs, they attempt to analyze the interrelationships among the processes of perception, imagery, symbolization, and conceptualization. At PEC, we often suspect these processes are skewed, making for at least some of the obstacles in the MLD's learning, as they try to move away from the direct experiences with the actual and concrete into the level of abstraction.

Much of the PEC population shows no obvious impairment, but many experts suspect that there is some damage within the sensory receptor. This could make it difficult for the MLD to receive and/or integrate the kinds of information that are divorced from direct experiences, particularly if the information is of a subtle or contradictory nature.

Experience in problem solving, then, is of critical importance to the MLD. In fact, in the teaching of *all* children and adults, whatever their age level and capacity, I have always been impressed with how much easier and better they learn if the approach is through exploration and experimentation. To tell fifth graders, or even a few college students, upon sight, that a pound of coal and a pound of feathers are the same pound, is confounding unless they themselves have had some direct experience with the weight process; without it, visual experience overrules judgment and submerges the fact.

In actuality, it takes the average child until he is about fourteen or fifteen years of age before he is able to arrive at the stage of abstract thinking wherein he can realize what is possible, without any reference to the concrete;

PROVERBS

AGE 8 YEARS *

A stitch in time saves nine
  it has a number, it rhymes

A rolling stone gathers no moss
  about rolling stones down a hill

Still water runs deep
  about water going down deep, some kind of water,
  not just plain water, don't know if people use it

A bird in the hand is worth two in the bush
  about holding one bird in your hand and a bush
  can hold two instead of one

Out of sight out of mind
  if something is out of sight it can't be in your mind

Don't count your chickens before they are hatched
  if you have chickens and count them before they are born
  you might make a mistake and they could be twins

* The eight-year-olds found it too difficult to answer in their own writing. The teacher recorded the answers and then typed them.

Proverbs

1. A stitch in time saves nine.
I think it means to take your time
in doing something so you don't have
to do it over again to take more time.

2. The wheel that squeaks gets the grease.
I am not so sure but I think it means
don't complain to much or you will
lose friends!

4. Don't count your chikkens before
they are hatched.
Don't think you can do something
when you can't.

5. Out of sight, out of mind.
I'm not sure but if people don't
like you they might say you're out
of sight and if they think you're
crazy you're out of mine.

6. A rolling stone gathers no moss.
I think it means if you're walking
around and a bunch of friends are
talking don't butt in.

① A stitch in time saves nine: A move at the right time might save lives.

② A rolling stone gathers no moss: A person who "two-times" gathers no friends.

③ Still water runs deep: Somebody who acts normal might have secrets inside.

④ A bird in the hand is better than two in the bush: Keep what you have and don't give it up for something that is better but that you might not get.

⑤ Out of sight out of mind: If you lose something, don't chase after it.

⑥ Don't count your chickens before their hatched: Don't be hasty.

ANONYMOUS
AGE: 14

What does it mean?

1. A stitch in time saves nine. If you do something now, it saves time later.

2. Still water runs deep. Even if someone dosen't show any feelings or emotions outside, deep inside they do have feeling -N- they do get hurt or happy.

3. A rolling stone gathers no moss. If one keeps moving around and doing something, one won't get tired of doing the same thing all the time.

4. Don't count your chickens before they hatch. Don't count on having things that you don't have yet because it might not work out the way you want it to

5. A birds in the hand is worth two in the bush Having something with you is worth more than two of that someplace else.

ANONYMOUS

AGE: 16

What does it mean?

1. A stitch in time saves nine.
   you can save something better when it is damaged a
   little but if you leave it to get worse. you would have
   to put in more time to gett it better or new

2. Still water runs deep.
   dont trust anyone ~~who look~~ by looks they might be hurt
   deep inside but looks calm

3. A rolling stone gathers no moss.
   if you are on the move all the time you would seldom
   settle down

4. Don't count your chickens before they hatch
   don't asume you would get something ~~before~~ you get
   it

5. A burd in the hand is worth two in the bush
   what you have is youre hand is youre but
   the two in the bush belongs to someone
   else. like what you have, not what other
   people have.

in other words before he can compare differences and similarities, generalize in a more than superficial way, and theorize. Arriving at such a stage, he is beginning to grasp the irony or the subtleties and apparent contradictions in the language of proverbs. This does not mean, though, that a fourteen- or fifteen-year-old's reasoning power is necessarily developed to its fullest, but that he usually has all the tools for thinking.

In teaching the MLD individual, there is no doubt that his difficulties in high-level abstracting will be lifelong. Fortunately, the 1950s saw an increased effort to improve the education of the learning disabled, albeit the concentration was on the lower IQs; but first steps in the betterment of the MLD's lot really began with the efforts of concerned parents' organizations. Nevertheless, despite the concerted efforts of them, and of many specialists, there has been and still is a lack of universal agreement concerning the reason for the MLD's learning problems. This gap has led to a challenge for teachers to deal with symptoms rather than causes. Under the circumstances, the value of an instructional program will depend on how effective its specific methods are in relieving identifiable learning problems, without respect to their etiology.

It has already been pointed out that the MLD individual's major learning impairment is his inability to cope with abstract problem-solving unless it is based on the concrete. Meeting the challenge to deal with symptoms, the PEC Program has been built around a fieldwork experience that enables its students to unscramble propositions through associating them with the reality of living. This is the kind of problem solving that is rarely made available to the MLD in an academic program; it is also closer to the kind that they meet up with in their daily lives; moreover, it is essential to the development of intelligence.

This experiential theory, expounded throughout the body of this book, is both critical and applicable to the MLD's development, from his preschool days throughout his adulthood.

VIEWING MENTAL GROWTH
WITH OPTIMISM

There is every reason to believe that parents and teachers can do a great deal to stimulate any child's social and cognitive growth early in life without violating the principles of human development. This does not include the view of those behaviorist followers who are setting the limits of the non-learning disabled child's cognitive expansion at the age of about two; they conclude that if the child has not had the fullest educational stimulation by toddlerhood, he will be lost to all other educational opportunities from then on.

There have been no results of long-range studies over the college years of these heavily-worked-over preschoolers; one may assume, then, that this dour conclusion is drawn from the knowledge we have about the stages within man's biological evolution. In these stages, there are critical periods for the various organs to develop. If one member misses its time of ascendancy, it is doomed, at the same time dooming the whole hierarchy of organs.

I view this analogy as entirely presumptive; I have been close to and taught some children whose young lives were educationally unstimulating, and consistently boring, yet who emerged as high-level intellectual adults; I have also witnessed the opposite phenomenon: intellectually stimulated very young children whose mental processes petered out as they moved up on the ladder into adulthood.

This is not meant to imply that there is not an optimal time for learning, often referred to as "readiness" by some educators—a concept that some behaviorists believe to be overrated; yet the idea of readiness is very much alive in their emphasis on the "critical stages" in learning, or referred to under the label of "sensitivity period."

We do know that children who are not verbally stimulated at the beginning will have serious problems in communication later on. Yet, with that as an exception, we have no knowledge about the *length* of critical time in academic learning, what subjects it applies to, and under what circumstances. My own work with children, covering nursery school years into adulthood, learning and non-learning disabled, convinces me that the learning possibilities of man are endless. It is also clear, at the same time, that many of the things we teach PEC young adults could have been more appropriately and profitably taught to them when they were young. Dr. George Orville Johnson charts the mental growth of the "slow learner," many of whom appear to be MLD, as follows:*

	Chronological Age		
IQ	6 Years	10 Years	15 Years
75 IQ	4 years 6 months	7 years 6 months	11 years 3 months
90 IQ	5 years 5 months	9 years	13 years 6 months

More to the point are the reports we receive from many of the examining psychologists concerning the test results of the PEC candidates when they were in the middle grades. There is an extreme inconsistency in the functioning of these perceptually handicapped children

* From George Orville Johnson, *Education for the Slow Learners* (Englewood Cliffs, N.J.: Prentice-Hall, 1963), p. 43

that makes it impossible to be confident about any final conclusions regarding the level of their intellectual operations. These youngsters can and often do perform above chronological age as well as one or more years below it. Some examiners believe that the intellectual process is so inconsistent that if a child were tested daily, he would produce vastly different results. Be that as it may, generally the tests place the MLD within the dull normal range of intelligence (approximately 75 to 90 IQ).

At PEC, we have been astonished at the progress of some of the students whose scores are on the lower end of the 75 to 95 IQ scale; in fact, some of the lower-standing students are finally more successful than some at the upper end, while those with approximately the same scores make different progress, depending on the nature of the handicap, the overall strengths, and the emotional tone of the individual. Besides, parents and teachers can take heart from the knowledge that no one has really seen the ceiling of the MLD child's cognitive ability, nor just what the reservoir of untapped resources are that he holds, particularly in a favorable setting.

None of this should distort the hard reality of the MLD's situation; their learning problems *are* more extreme and pervasive, but the MLD have a great plus in their sharing of the overall human qualities common to all children. An awareness, therefore, of the norms of the child's development, as diagrammed by the Drapers' Chart (pages 68–70), as well as the means to implement it as set forth in this book, will guide parents and teachers in helping the MLD child's expansion. The PEC Program, built upon the extrapolation of work with the non-learning disabled, has not only been highly successful in the education and training of MLD young adults, but, it turns out, has all kinds of implications for teaching the MLD throughout childhood.

DRAPERS' CHART

MOTOR DEVELOPMENT—INFANCY

Birth to 3 months

Smiles spontaneously
Lifts head when supported at shoulders
Holds head steady without support
Responds to bell or rattle
Reaches

3 to 5 months

Smiles in response to others
Smiles at mirror image
Laughs
Rolls over
Holds head steady and erect when in a sitting position
Uses arms and hands in reaching
Uses both hands to grasp object offered
Crawling movements begin

5 to 9 months

Squeals with joy or pleasure
Transfers an object from one hand to the other
Reaches and grasps toy
Sits without support
Holds two toys or cubes
Creeps and crawls
Can self-feed with finger foods
Stands with support

6 to 12 months

Pulls up to sitting position without help
Stands by holding on to something
Crawls or moves on stomach or in a sitting position without walking
Uses thumb and finger for grasping
Self-feeds with food items such as crackers
Pulls and pushes toys and objects
Imitates speech sounds

9 to 15 months

Stands alone
Walks while holding on to something
Looks at pictures in baby picture book
Plays with blocks

11 to 15 months

Walks alone in a toddling fashion
Climbs on furniture
Grasps small objects with thumb and finger
Imitates words
Holds cup and bottle alone
Drinks from a cup
Shows right or left handedness

12 to 18 months

Turns pages of a book
Can say about three words
Builds tower of two cubes
Scribbles spontaneously

14 to 17 months

Runs
Throws ball overhand without control of direction
Uses spoon; spills easily
Points to parts of face—nose, ear, eye, mouth, chin
Points to parts of doll—hair, mouth, hands, feet
Uses words to make wants known

15 to 22 months

Walks up steps with help
Walks backwards
Removes simple items of clothing
Eats with a spoon
Builds tower of three cubes
Carries and hugs doll or stuffed animal
First tooth with biting and chewing replaces mouthing and gumming

DRAPERS' CHART

(*Continued*)

MOTOR DEVELOPMENT—EARLY CHILDHOOD

18 to 30 months

Walks up steps alone
Recognizes and points to
    pictures
Makes sentences of two or three
    words
Manipulates push and pull toys
    easily
Stacks and lines up blocks
Turns pages with ease
Tears paper
Puts finger into holes
Waves "by-by"
Begins taking things apart
Can undress self

2 to 3 years

Runs
Climbs on various objects such
    as furniture and stairs
Kicks ball forward
Throws ball overhand but
    without aiming
Unwraps and removes covers
    from candy or other items,
    such as peeling banana
Takes simple objects apart with
    little difficulty
Unfastens clothing
Runs, jumps, tumbles, hops
Jumps and hops with one foot
    leading
Climbs stairs with two feet on
    each step
Throws balls of various sizes
Turns pages with ease
Puts fingers in openings and
    holes
Turns knobs by rotating wrist
Constructs towers by stacking
    several blocks
Scribbles up and down and
    across
Holds cup and glass with control

Eats with a spoon
Begins self-dressing with
    independence
Can undress with ease

3 to 4 years

Runs, jumps, hops, skips, gallops
Climbs and descends stairs
Slides in skating and dancing
    motions
Can march to rhythm
Rolls and crawls on floor
Balances self on one foot
Kicks balls
Jumps over a rope
Pedals wheel toys
Touches toes
Can do sit-ups, chin-ups, and
    push-ups
Throws and bounces a ball
Catches a ball or a bean bag
Pulls and pushes objects
Strings beads
Stands on one foot for a short
    time
Builds with blocks
Cuts with scissors
Uses large crayons and pencils
Rolls wrists and closes fists
Cuts out assorted shapes with
    scissors
Can fold paper
Screws and unscrews objects
Draws directed lines and
    scribbling
Manipulates puzzles with few to
    several pieces
Manipulates simple objects by
    putting parts which require
    little skill together
Draws a circle—usually from a
    model
Builds a tower of eight cubes—
    usually from a model

DRAPERS' CHART
(Continued)

MOTOR DEVELOPMENT—EARLY CHILDHOOD
(Continued)

3 to 4 years (cont.)

Manipulates spoon and fork for self-feeding

Dresses with success except for tying shoes, bows, and manipulating some fasteners

---

4 to 5 years

Climbs play equipment—jungle gym, towers, slides, and ladders

Balances on one foot

Catches and throws 3-, 5-, and 12-inch balls

Bounces and catches balls

Hops on both feet

Hops on one foot—four steps

Skips in unison to music

Skips rope

Participates vigorously in outdoor play

Rides wheel toys with speed and skill

Balances on beam or board

Manipulates buttons, zippers, and may tie bows

Threads beads or spools on string

Plays jacks

Pounds and rolls clay

Forms crude and some recognizable objects with clay

Places blocks horizontally on floor

Stacks blocks vertically

Creates recognizable structures with blocks

Participates in finger plays

Controls crayons, pencils, paint brushes, chalk

Understands and uses scissors

Can follow line when cutting with scissors

Cuts and pastes according to directions

Maintains rhythmic beat with rhythm band and instruments

Joins in games requiring group movement such as circles and dancing

Places pegs in pegboard

Builds structures with Tinkertoys

Uses real hammer and saw in simple woodworking activity

Can pour from a small pitcher into a glass

Can hold and eat with spoon or fork correctly

Can use knife to cut food

Turns corners and about-face

Self-dresses with ease

Enjoys large-muscle activity— running, tumbling, climbing, fast-moving activities involving the whole body

---

SOURCE: Mary Wanda Draper and Henry E. Draper, *Caring For Children*, Chas. A. Bennett Co., Inc., Peoria, Illinois, 1975
NOTE: Such differences and overlapping stages as there may be reflect the need for flexibility in using any diagram as a guide; while the children's rates of development share many things in common, no pace is the same.

MOTIVATION: THE NUB OF LEARNING

Beginning at birth, motivation appears to be indigenous to the human organism. It is apparent in the child's curiosity about the objects around him, his drive to explore, and the pleasure he takes in the sheer doing of an exercise that lies within his command.

In school, one of the reasons this natural thrust becomes spoiled for a great many pupils is because their classroom experiences have been taken up by too much meaningless activity. Upon being confronted by the frequent question PEC observers ask—"How do your young adults learn after so many years of failure?"—we answer, "motivation."

Loreen was clearly an example of this. By age sixteen, ill-tempered and frustrated, she had closed herself in her room, rarely consenting to do anything or go anywhere; television was her sole companion. But her parents often turned their thoughts to the times when she would befriend some younger children in the neighborhood, so, when they read about PEC, they convinced her to give it a try.

At first Loreen presented many problems, but like a plant straightening up after it has been given enough water, she began to thrive. As she learned to trust the caring staff, many of her fears gradually evaporated; and as she gained in confidence, and the sweet part of her nature began to assert itself, the staff came to love her. The PEC Program, which allowed Loreen to use her drive to become an aide in the helping professions, guided her to her success.

71

Mervin was another example of what motivation can do for one under the right circumstances. He was born into a well-to-do family; sadly, both of his parents had grown exasperated by his long series of school failures. But in his older brother, ten years his senior and a clinical psychologist, he found consistent support and sympathy.

After Mervin struggled through years of failure in a good private school, his brother finally succeeded in having him shifted to a high school for exceptional children, from which he earned a certificate. Its report stated, among other things, that, "He is a nice boy, but completely lacking in self-confidence, and he gives up very easily." His achievement tests put his academic standing between the fourth and sixth grades.

Upon graduation, Mervin's father got two jobs for him, the first in a packaging room and the second as an errand boy. Mervin got fired from both of them. From then on he stayed home, slept late, looked at TV, and remained listless and downhearted.

One Thanksgiving Day, Mervin's brother, who had just married, had his family to dinner along with another couple who were close friends. They brought with them their four-year-old son, Tod. Restless and mischievous as Tod was, the psychologist brother asked Mervin if he wouldn't take Tod outside and watch him as he ran around and "let off steam." About an hour later, when the older brother went out to fetch them, as he told me, "I just stood transfixed. Mervin was teaching Tod to catch a ball, and his interest, kindness and patience astounded me. I'd heard about the PEC Program," he went on, "but I never dreamed Merv would be interested. In fact I wondered if he could be interested in *anything*."

Once Mervin came to PEC, his motivation for helping young children led him to be one of our most successful students both in his PEC studies and at the nursery school. After graduation he was hired by a school where he is a teacher aide, an errand boy, and where he does all of the odd jobs at hand. Meanwhile, he has come alive.

Even when circumstances are far from perfect, given the inducement, the possibilities for human growth are endless.

THE NEED FOR ORDER

In an earlier phase of the history of education, teachers knew little about the child's mental development; they simply regarded themselves as vehicles for teaching the child certain subjects that would enable him to *think*. Subject matter was the mainspring of a well-defined program around which the child's school personality shaped itself; and whatever the faults of the school, the studies were treated with respect and as essential tools for brainwork. All children, handicapped or otherwise, who are not taught to think, remain uncivilized; often they are wild. One of the best illustrations of this point is the dramatic experience in the childhood of that remarkable blind-mute, Helen Keller.

By the time Helen was seven, her teacher, Anne Sullivan, with stupendous effort, had taught Helen eighteen nouns and three verbs; but the child's grasp of those words was through rote memorization, without any basic understanding. Her responses, therefore, were mechanical; milk meant to drink. She was unable to realize milk was a liquid among many other liquids. Neither could she compare it, nor generalize about it; put simply, she really didn't have the means to think effectively.

To live in a world in which one cannot manage to use

73

one's mind is to live with very little understanding; it leaves one without any order, and without any means to cope or master. In Helen's world, she was like a moth beating its wings against a powerful light—and she was wild.

One day Miss Sullivan took the girl out to the pump house. Helen held her mug under the spout while her teacher pumped out the cool liquid, meanwhile tapping "w-a-t-e-r" in Helen's free hand. Sensing the very cold fluid, as it spilled onto her hand, probably gave Helen the shock of recognition. Her entire being underwent an almost instant metamorphosis; suddenly she was able to extract the essence of the liquid and shape it into the symbol, or the word, "water." She now had the idea to think about, and to enlarge upon. Water was not only to drink; she would soon be able to realize that it was also a liquid, hot or cold; it could be found in streams, lakes, and the ocean; it could be bathed in. Eventually the child would be able to specify, compare differences and similarities; and she could generalize.

Helen had found the magic key; it opened up a lifetime flow of endless ideas, as it does for all human beings, helping to shape herself and her world into a unified whole. Although the etiology of this child's learning disability was obviously different, I think it very likely that the frenetic behavior of many brain-damaged and mentally deficient youngsters is similar to the kind of turmoil that Helen felt; individuals who are unable to conceptualize are without the kind of reason that helps to put themselves and their world into order.

LOVE IN TEACHING

Miss Sullivan was not unconcerned about love, but her love was a means to an end. Her dogged objectivity in pursuing her educational goals stands out in striking contrast to the attitudes of many educators, whose schools, a few generations later, became centered around the child's emotional needs. In the 1950s the director of such a school became one of my doctoral candidates. Part of his hypothesis was that a child will learn the three Rs through love and self-expression—never mind if that meant throwing mud in someone's face. His was the A. S. Neill approach, in which study is optional. Keeping the child "happy" is the main goal. Like Neill, my candidate had not the slightest interest in nor knowledge of the child's mental functioning, nor the teacher's training toward that goal. "I care about the child's feelings," he said. "They're the only thing that matters. Teachers who know how to feel, know how to teach."

I thought about Miss Sullivan and her constant search for the tools and techniques that would open up Helen's mind. No one could have felt or cared more, but her caring grew out of an adulthood that had put its toys away, and from that height, she could view her frantic pupil with an objectivity that separated her own needs from her student's.

One takes for granted that any teacher who works with children, MLD or otherwise, cares about them; but the fundamental difference between the teacher and the parent is that the teacher's training and his professional techniques are *his* particular assets for reaching the

75

child. They also help him to maintain a valuable distance that allows for an objective approach.

In working with teachers I've observed that the less resourceful they are as professionals, the more overinvolved with the student they are likely to become, leaning more on personal appeal than on the tools of the trade. For example, at PEC, most students show a good deal of their vulnerability as they struggle with weak academic skills. Even the able professional, in working with this population, invites trouble with the leading yesor-no question of, "Don't you want to improve?"

Almost inevitably our students respond with a blank stare, or the complaint, "I've had it all my life and it's a waste of time"; or, "I'm sick and tired of it"; or, "It never helped me."

Upon the inquiry "Why?" or "How come?" there follows a gush of blame on parents, teachers, siblings, or whoever fits into the MLD's picture. As the teacher probes further, up comes more emotion; in fact, youngsters easily become self-righteous and irreconcilable the more they are encouraged to explain the reasons for their inadequacy in such situations; and while their anger may well be justified, anger feeds on anger, with no positive results.

Now the teacher realizes that, whatever the problems, the learning disability itself needs to be tackled. His kind, supportive approach also needs firmness and courage to help cut through the web of feelings. This takes both the professional's skills and the child's own responsibility, including the consequences of his behavior.

"Don't you want to improve your reading?" (for example) must give way to something like, "I'm here to help you improve your reading and I want to show you how; your job is to try to improve if you want to earn a diploma and get a job as a teacher aide."

If the student is well-motivated, however resistfully

and grudgingly at first, he will take the opportunity; if he doesn't, the teacher must ask himself some penetrating questions; in this case, is the student in the right place? On the right level? Is the work beyond his scope? Are the teacher's skills adequate?

Most MLD are well-motivated; they are earnest and eager to learn, whatever their learning limitations are. With suitable tools, methods, and techniques, the imaginative, sympathetic teacher can remain objective in his help; through that objectivity, the MLD is more likely to receive the kind of love his mind can grow on.

3

Helping the Young MLD Child Learn Through Experience

A HEAD START

A head start is always an advantage. It doesn't take a wizard to know that children who are provided with good educational opportunities early in life are usually further ahead. As I mentioned earlier, it is apparent to those of us who teach at PEC that our young MLD adults, most of whom have come from caring homes, could have learned many of the elementary facts we must now teach them much earlier in their primary- and elementary-school life, not only from their teachers, but their parents as well.

Studies (such as Piaget's) of the relationship between experience and intelligence reveal that, from the very beginning, a child's mind develops as his body and behavior expand. The pattern of his mental growth is integrated within the broad areas of adaptive behavior (this, among other things, includes perceiving relationships, and the involvement of sensory-motor activities essential to problem solving and thinking); gross and fine motor behavior; visible and audible language behavior; and personal and social behavior.

In the growth of the baby, there is a natural and gradual unfolding of his native capacities. However, there is more to learning than this development, as the socially and intellectually isolated and very disadvantaged child has demonstrated. A muscle grows weak and becomes wasted when it remains unused; correspondingly, if the child is to make the fullest use of his verbal skills, he must be talked to and he must talk himself.

All of the infant's motor and sensory organs are primary ways to his development; tasting, touching, smelling, seeing, and hearing are profoundly important as he learns to carry out the simplest movement, from which, very gradually, thinking, learning, and communicating develop. So it is of great value for parents to encourage the child to exercise his sensory powers, as he takes his first steps, however small, toward problem solving and the generating of an idea.

Infants, of course, should not be bombarded by parents, well meaning as their intentions may be; no brain can be quickly transformed into an adult's by excessive sensory stimulation and drill. But in the proper interest of the child, probably too few people are conscious of the numerous ways, in the natural context of daily life, that they can help him achieve a richer social and cognitive existence, be he learning disabled or not.

The baby's daily physical activity, when he is being supported and bathed, for example, provides a good opportunity for the infant's budding, while he thrashes and splashes in the water, feels the liquid, and plays with his toys. Simple equipment that the child can eye, taste, chew, rattle, bang, and manipulate, as he lies on his blanket, or when he is cuddled and fondled, turned over and spoken to, will help the baby explore and interact with his immediate environment, by sharpening and expanding his powers of perception, and stimulating his cognitive powers.

Parents who can avoid treating their baby as if he were a push-button mechanical doll who must be made to respond to a chart of averages will profit from using the Drapers' framework (see pages 68–70). Showing the child's development across the broad range of age levels as the chart does suggests the kind of appropriate experiences with which parents can provide the infant. Whatever kinds of incentive adults provide for the MLD and the non-learning disabled child, it is likely that the attitude and manner of the adult who intervenes are as germane to the child's well-being as the intervention itself; in some instances, the attitude may be more important. For the infant's gradual realization of his surroundings is closely interwoven with the way in which the adult meets the child's physical and emotional needs.

The MLD will be slower than the average child in learning; at the same time, such a child will have many strengths he can call on. Loving and stable parents who can accept him with whatever handicaps he shows will help him to establish feelings of basic trust and self-confidence. Feelings of mistrust, born out of a conflicting attitude toward the baby, or a stormy, stressful atmosphere, may be modified later, but some scars from early childhood may remain throughout life. Fortunately, the human being possesses extraordinary strengths, as we see in most of our MLD young adults, despite their past hardships; and he can manage reasonably well with much less than perfection. Indeed, it may reassure parents to realize that the child could hardly cope with the real world without learning to cope throughout his growing-up period with its inevitable strains and tribulations.

GROWING UP TAKES TIME

Parents can easily be thrown off the track by some of the fairly recent literature about the very young child's development, especially in the cognitive area, wherein he is often portrayed as a miniature adult.

Early clinicians, with Freud as the leading figure, set great store by the influence on his later life of the child's first two or three years. In *The First Five Years of Life*, now considered a classical study, Dr. Gesell and his group were the first to provide a step-by-step guide to the infant's unfoldings. The first two years are even more painstakingly spelled out, phase by phase, with some good practical suggestions for stimulating the baby's social and cognitive processes in Burton White's *The First Three Years of Life*.

But caution is needed, in reading some of the recent literature, when considering the authors' interpretations of the baby's surface behavior. It is as easy to read the wisdom of Solomon in the child's earliest verbal expressions as it is to underestimate the things the child takes in before he can talk. Often we are startled by some utterance of the child's because we expect to hear so little; or we are likely to interpret it in the light of our own adult comprehension, instead of realizing that a two- or three-year-old can comprehend only in the light of his two- or three-year-old mental development and experience, however bright he may be.

Just as Freud opened up an entirely new view to our comprehension of the young child's feelings, so Piaget has added new dimensions to our understanding of his cognitive development. His studies leave little doubt that

physical and mental growth follow a predetermined sequence in all children, and that the developmental stages
cannot be profitably skipped or pushed beyond readiness. As Piaget illustrates it, it takes nine to twelve
months before babies (if they are not drilled) can realize
that an object is still present when a screen has been
placed before it; a kitten arrives at the same knowledge
at about the age of three months. Piaget claims that the
nine months undoubtedly have a reason since, although
the child comes to it more slowly, he goes much further
in the end.

Piaget's ingenuity is most visible as he reveals how different in quality from the adult's the child's reasoning
process is. Yet, there are those who will judge by the
child's external behavior alone, as they fall prey to their
own wishful thinking. These individuals tell us that at
age one, the child is a thinker, at age two, a truly social
being, that at age three he can hold a conversation with
his parents as if they were his peers—a cryptic statement
to say the least—and that by age six, he can grasp the
meaning of time by knots tied in a string.

But tuning into the preschooler's inner processes picks
up a different story. One thing that prevents him from
being able to function on an adult level is his animistic
view, through which he sees things and objects as having
the same motives, feelings, and actions as his own; he is
unable to grasp objective cause-and-effect relationships.
So, it is futile to attempt formal explanations based on a
logic that is distant from the child's way of thinking. A
three-year-old will most likely shake his head in agreement when you tell him that somebody did not throw
the leaves on the ground, but that the wind did it; and he
can easily repeat what he has been told verbatim. However, in the same breath, he may tell you that, "Now the
moon is woke up"; or, as he pours water down the drain,
"See, it goes down the ear"; or, upon banging his head

against the corner of the table, he spanks it, saying, "Bad table," as if it deliberately hurt him.

Connected with the young child's animistic thinking is his confusion about what is real and what is fantasy or make-believe. Until about age five, the child makes a poor audience for the magician, seeing nothing strange about a rabbit coming out of a hat.

Young children also have a hard time keeping more than one view in mind at the same time. A three-year-old child, not recognizing his teacher outside of school, asked, "What is your name with your hat on?" (That is not so farfetched as it may seem; I saw a fifth-grade class unable to take in the fact that it was still their teacher who came to school one day with his completely bald head topped with a wig.)

As is common, another three-year-old, approaching a sixty-year-old supervisor, who was observing her student teacher in his class, asked, "Whose mommy are you?"

A girl of four, when being asked, "Do you have a brother?" replied, "Yes," but upon being asked, "Does your brother have a sister?" replied, "No." In typical fashion she was unable to comprehend two views at the same time.

Although not completely resolved, there is an expansion in outlook when the child is five. In a nursery school, the following conversation took place:

GEORGE: "I love you, Jana."
JANA: "I love you, too, George."
GEORGE: "Do you love anyone else, Jana?"
JANA: "Yes, I love Helen, George [the one being addressed], Jenny, and me."
GEORGE: "You love yourself, Jana?"
JANA: "Yes, I love me. You could love yourself."

And for a long time, young children see a symbol as something having its own life, with a name, color, and form being intrinsic to it. A child about four and a half,

83

upon hearing his mother exclaim, "Oh, figs!" said, "Figs are to eat. They're brown and seedy."

One is likely to overestimate the cognitive powers of children in the early middle grades, too, unless one listens carefully, for they reason about things and not propositions. Try telling a first grader, "Let's pretend the snow is red." There is usually some indignation as the child insists that it is white.

These primary-grade children, being very literal, are not able to deal with metaphor, nor can they read between the lines. It will take them until their teens before they can do so. (See pages 57–63.)

Piaget emphasises how much all children need to be allowed to live and relive experiences, as they seek the right answers; they need to explore and experiment through trial and error, while they enlarge upon their findings. When facts are poured into a child, he misses the valuable opportunity to retrace his steps and examine what he has heard and seen; he becomes like a tree, that, hemmed in by sparse facts, grows too quickly to the sun, without its full width of branches.

Gesell was probably right when he said, almost fifty years ago, that it takes an American youth about twenty years to reach the stature of adulthood. He, of course, was focusing on the interrelationship of physical, mental, and social growth—the kind of maturity essential to the well-being of all human beings, learning handicapped or not. In any case, growing up takes a long time.

EARLY LANGUAGE DEVELOPMENT

A child will not talk until he is ready, nor can he be pushed into the act, but he can be stimulated in the process, and that is fundamental to his maturation.

Parents of MLD children can profit from the realization that toddlerhood is commonly the time when the child is walking and into language development. For the average child this is roughly between about fifteen to sixteen months to about two and a half years old; the MLD is likely to be slower, however.

Learning disabled or not, a child learns to talk through imitation, association, example, and experience. He must hear the verbal, and be invited to respond. Once the child begins to converse, parents may see him as an intellectual, or, on the other hand, they may believe he is too young to be taken seriously. Instead, if parents could realize how much all children take in, they would be more careful of the kinds of things they say to each other, either about them, or about affairs that are inappropriate for their ears, as if they did not exist. Still, there is a great deal children hear that they do not understand.

If parents of the MLD can recognize how complex comprehension of ideas is behind non-learning disabled children's use of words, they may be more alert to the confusions of the MLD, with their greater dependence on memorization, and their need for the concrete to mirror the meaning.

The serious remarks of non-learning disabled children that follow below will reveal the muddled stages in their comprehension:

A two-year-old, after visiting a zoo, told his professor grandfather, "I saw an okapi [an animal related to a giraffe] at the zoo today."

"An okapi?"

"Yes," shouting as if his grandfather were deaf, "an okapi."

"What's an okapi?"

"An animal."

"I never heard of one."

"Huh. An okapi. It's spelled, 'z-o-o!' " Triumphantly.

A teacher, talking to a child about his manner of speaking to another child said, "Try not to be a grouch."

Another two-year-old corrected her: "He's a boy."

A three-year-old in school, having been told a friend has a cold, turned to another child. "How cold are you?" she asked.

As some three-year-olds were observing the gerbils, one remarked, "I like to 'nice' the gerbils."

At another time a three-year-old commented to a friend, "When they grow up and get bigger, my mommy and daddy will get married, if they want to."

A child, almost four, after his nursery class named its gerbil "Bumblebee," went home and told his mother that the class had a tuna in the cage.

Another child of about the same age, when told that people go to the Statue of Liberty by ferryboat, responded, "How can a boat be a 'fairy'? Fairies fly; they are not boats."

In a group of fours, at the beginning of the year, the children were not always driven home by the same bus driver. One of the children who was concerned about this was assured that the bus driver would always know where he lived and would take him to his own home. He then replied, "Oh, and will I go home to the same mommy?"

Another time Laura and Peter were talking about how they would marry when they grew up.

Peter: "I will go to work and you will have the babies and take care of them." Laura answered that *she* would like to go to work. "OK," Peter said, "you go to work and I'll have the babies."

Another anecdote of fours, involving the use of words and the comprehension of ideas:

A: "Sometimes my mommy puts me in my room and I yell at her."

B: "If you really want to get rid of her, why don't you throw her out of the window?"

C: "Oh, no, you can't do that: first it's not nice, she's too big for you, and your daddy will fire you if you do that."

In the housekeeping corner of the five-year-old kindergarten class the following conversation was heard:

Mother: "Put the baby to sleep."

Father: "The baby is not tired."

Mother: "Well, put him to sleep anyhow; you know babies are supposed to take naps."

Father: "Yeah, my mother told me I used to take a nap."

Mother: "So, baby, go to sleep."

At lunchtime, to the teacher, a five said, "You know why I won't eat?"

"No, tell me."

"Well, when I eat I get bigger and bigger. When I'm old then I'll die."

"Well, I ate and grew and grew and didn't die. You can eat and grow and grow old and you don't have to worry about dying."

"No? Are you sure?"

"Yes, I'm very sure."

The child ate her lunch and enjoyed it, for she had been quite hungry.

A bright six, upon being told that she was wearing a beautiful carnation, looked blank. "What's a carnation?"

"The flower you're wearing."

"Oh."

A second-grade teacher, whose hair was beginning to turn gray at the top of her head, was asked by her seven-year-old pupil, "Are people born with gray hair?"

The teacher of a fifth grade of ten- to eleven-year-olds was dismissing her class for the Christmas recess. She was thirty-one years of age.

"Where are you going?" one child asked her.

"To Florida to see my parents."

"*You* have parents?"

Another time, unrelated to the Florida incident, one of the children asked her, "How old are you?"

"Guess."

One pupil said eighteen, another fifty, and another sixty.

The MLD who has rich personal experiences is likely to be more verbal. Like all children, his first words will be about his concrete experiences within his daily life activities. Depending upon where he lives, his excursions and experiences, discussed below, will stimulate his thinking and provide topics for his comments and conversation.

If the child can have indoor and outdoor space available, with appropriate materials and equipment (See Appendix, pages 223–224), activities employing these things will help stimulate his verbalization. Youngsters particularly enjoy playing house with adult dress-up clothes, dolls, toy animals, and miniature kitchen provisions—and are likely to do so until about the third grade, at least, if they are left on their own.

Healthy sources for language development also lie in the handwork of drawing, painting, clay work, cutting, pasting, sewing, puppetry, and so on. Moreover, these activities, essential for the MLD, help build inner resources early in life—the best time for the habit to take hold. These occupations can grow out of anything dramatic and unusual in your child's existence—special events like holidays, birthday celebrations, picnics, and the like.

And family jobs that the child can handle will move him to converse. He can begin with putting some toys away, picking up items of clothes, and taking a dish to the sink—jobs that are nothing to the adult, but help the youngster feel worthwhile.

Story reading is another valuable asset in language development. That includes looking at and cutting out pictures, while making simple comments and asking simple questions, if they are needed to get the child involved. Story dictation is also a help. A four-year-old non-learning disabled child, when asked to tell a story (which the parent or teacher should write down), will take it out of his daily life, in which almost any occurrence is great news: "Yesterday my daddy took me to the zoo. He bought me an ice-cream cone." The story should be printed in large letters that are easy to read, and on a big sheet of paper that can be tacked up on the wall.

Seeing his account on the home or school bulletin board is pleasing to the child in that he gains self-respect, with the idea that an adult has found it worthwhile to write down something *he* said. In addition to the feeling of encouragement he gets in communicating, he reflects on past events as he tells about them—a process of thinking—as well as getting a sense of letter and word formation, when his story is being written down.

Recording the youngster's stories in manuscript, or printed letters, follows the storybook method; this is an easier way to the beginning of reading and writing for the young child.

For the MLD who has an especially hard time getting a thought out, Mrs. Angel used this technique with her five-year-old Rowena:

"Tomorrow we're visiting Cousin Mabel, Rowena."

"I'll ride on the swings," Rowena said.

"Let's make a story out of that," Mrs. Angel said, getting the paper and pencil that she had at her elbow. "Now what are we going to do tomorrow, Rowena?"

"Visit Mabel."

Mrs. Angel said the words as she wrote, "Tomorrow we will visit Mabel."

"What did you say you would do there, Rowena?"

"Ride on the swings."

Mrs. Angel added that thought, again saying each word as she wrote it. Then she had Rowena read the story aloud with her, as she pointed to the words:

"Tomorrow we will visit Mabel. I will ride on the swings."

Most MLD need to be spoken to clearly and simply, using words that are unequivocal in meaning. Adults customarily get the implication of a strange word through the context, but for the MLD child, who usually has more than the average amount of trouble with the meaning of new words, a way-out interpretation may strike him as right, thus increasing his confusion. This was well illustrated when Mr. Dorn asked his son, almost six, who knew where the electric bulbs were kept, to "get an electric light bulb from the closet."

Mr. Dorn knew that there were only 60-watt bulbs left, so he figured that his son would have no problem. But John took so long to return that his father finally went to fetch him. He found his son standing with a light bulb in each hand, looking down at the others.

"I don't see any 'light,' " John said.

Later, Mr. Dorn remarked to me that, "In teaching John how to communicate, I'm learning myself."

ROUTINE AND SCHEDULE

All children need a steady routine of activities and a time schedule; the MLD child needs this regularity even more, and it is essential throughout his adult life, as well. In fact, consider what happens to the non-learning disabled adult when the pattern of his days suddenly changes; he asks, "What day is it?" Often he feels lost without the usual reckoning of his life-style. The necessity of this feed-back has been emphasized by experiments; in one, individuals closed-off in a room for a long period of time, without any stimulus, became completely disoriented.

As early as age three and a half in a well-planned nursery school class, if the regular teacher is absent, and the substitute is uncertain of the procedure, or tries to change it, some children will be sure to set him straight with some correction like, "But we don't go to the roof now; it's snack time." One of the main reasons that a class of children, right up through the grades, is likely to be consistently frenetic is the lack of any regular routine or schedule.

Wherever the MLD child is, he should be helped to realize a routine and schedule (see Appendix, page 225). Once the youngster is walking and talking, parents can help him to become conscious of the regular events that balance his day: "It is eight o'clock in the morning, and time for your breakfast"; or, "Now that you have had your lunch, it is time for your nap"; or, "It is after two o'clock now and time to go out and play." The MLD child may not be able to read clock time before he is seven or eight, but the personal time of the day's activities gives the clock more meaning.

Noting calendar time further helps the MLD child's orientation: "It's a cold winter's day, so wear your heavy coat." "There's lots of snow on the ground now that it's January." "It's always hotter in the summer months." "Tomorrow is Saturday, the day we visit Grandma." "Tomorrow is Sunday, the day we go to church." "June twelfth. It's your birthday." These kinds of comments prepare the way for understanding the calendar which is a complicated matter for children. This is exemplified by a child not yet four who said, "My sister's birthday was tomorrow"; or another four-year-old who insisted, "It's not 'today'! My mommy said it was Monday."

There should be occasional changes in the regular routine and schedule, of course, to help the child build in some needed flexibility, as well as enlarging his horizon; but he needs notice of the upcoming event a few hours or perhaps a day or so in advance, depending on his age and the circumstances. The child is likely to forget a too early notice, or if the event is unusual, such as a birthday, or Christmas, the excitement can build up too far in advance. In any case, the MLD's sense of orientation in time and space—both of which also deal indirectly with number—is aided by the day's regularity.

PATIENCE

When Mrs. Horrane told the parents of some MLD, "Calvin [age four and a half] takes forever to dress. It's really a pain. I hurry him up, but it doesn't do any good," the discussion turned to the immense amount of patience *all* young children need.

In everyday procedures, it helps to realize that time is meaningless to youngsters; except as it affects their needs, they seldom see any reason to hurry. It is one thing to prod the child when an appointment must be kept on time, or to help the child who obviously cannot get his arm through the sleeve, or has difficulty with buttons; but the impatient adult, who habitually grabs and shoves articles of clothing on the child, or takes possession of the two-year-old's spoon to feed him, is letting the child know that there is no faith in his ability to manage on his own, thus undermining his confidence.

The MLD, in efforts that may be fumbling, can spill or drop things; he may also be more forgetful at points than the child who is not learning disabled. An occasional show of impatience is inevitable; generally, though, it is easier for the child to take when it is displayed within a casual and accepting attitude. As Mrs. Salwyn said, "I tell Mark [age five] a little ahead of time that we've got to get to the dentist and he can't dawdle. When he doesn't cooperate at times like that, I get mad. He puts up with my anger because when there's no reason to rush I let him take all the time he needs."

SOCIAL DEVELOPMENT THROUGH PLAY

The young child who is just getting on his feet is obviously not ready for peer friendships. Social contacts, starting about age three, are usually a matter of side-by-side play, or copying each other. Nevertheless, it is healthy for the child to enlarge his circle with even that casual kind of relationship.

In many cultures today, if the preschooler is the only youngster in the neighborhood, his best chances for peer relationships will be in day-care or the nursery school setting. There, with his peers, he is exposed to a much greater variety of materials and equipment, and their accompanying activity.

While the play of the various age levels is anything but cut-and-dried, some generalizations can be made. That of the fours tends to be informal, with group members constantly shifting in and out. Although these children can and do cooperate with each other, the materials and equipment tend to dictate the kind of play they will have. The children do not tend to be competitive, although they show intense feelings of affection and anger, much of which usually lasts only a very short time.

Five-year-old play in many ways resembles that of the six-year-old. It continues to be extremely energetic and exploratory, but the newfound skills help these children to make things for a purpose, and to build upon the play of the preceding years. The process is still the important thing, however; if the child is not influenced, he will show little interest in winning. Household play and trying on roles are very active during this period.

THE FREEING AGENT OF SELF-CONTROL

Had Mrs. Franz understood more about children's social development, she might have been able to take her five-year-old son's behavior a bit more philosophically. "I can't bear to take Jo to the sandbox," she told a parents' group. "He grabs the other boys' pails, or hits them over the head with his shovel, or God knows what. I get in there fast enough and yell at him to stop it or I'll spank him. Finally I get so desperate that I take him home and shut him up in his room. But it doesn't do any good. He screams and throws everything on the floor until in desperation I let him out. Then he is more wild than ever. So I spank him some more, and then I'm sick with myself altogether. It's a terrible situation."

Mrs. Franz was greatly relieved to learn that most five-year-old children, MLD or not, tend to be very active and aggressive in their play. Mrs. Lake asked her if she ever let the children fight it out, saying, "Another child might teach him a lesson better than you can."

"But, I'm embarrassed in front of other parents," was Mrs. Franz's reply. Again, wisely, Mrs. Lake suggested that "it might be more helpful to Jo if *another* parent scolded him"; or, "If the other children refuse to play with him, that would teach him a good lesson."

Unless danger is involved, aside from removing him from the situation, it is better to wait and talk with the child when things have calmed down. Then he needs to be told: "That is not the way to behave toward others"; or, "You wouldn't like it if a child did that to you."

Let the punishment—a word we should not be afraid of—be brief and moderate; a little for the adult is a lot for the child. The purpose is not to make the child vindictive and angry with you so that he will forget his responsibility for the difficulty and want to pay you back, thus making for a vicious circle; what he needs is to be relieved from the pesky situation that induced his faulty behavior in the first place. Allow him to feel his error as he cools off; being sent to a quiet room, for a few moments, with a picture book, or crayons and paper, blocks, or any playthings that will divert him, is often the best treatment.

Diversion and redirection are the healthiest techniques for helping the child to get off the nuisance track; if he is unable to work it out alone, be ready to read a story to him, show him some pictures, or get on the floor into the block building yourself. Self-control or self-discipline is much more easily promoted if we learn to engage in worthwhile interests that sublimate our anger.

It takes many years for most any child to develop mature self-control; he goes through a number of stages on the way before he can *fully* share, give and take, stop and go, and do things for others, as well as for himself. By the time he is eleven or twelve, though, his ability to get along should be reasonably steady, but along the way he will need help, and much patience and support in the process.

Children quickly forgive the adult whose censure may be excessive or unfair, if his overall feeling is one of basic trust. It is the gestalt—the whole pattern—that affects him most. In that context, the example the adult sets is of primary importance—probably much more important than the verbal directives. In the end, reasonable adults are likely to have reasonable children.

A hard job for parents? Infinitely hard, yes. For the adult must cope not only with his own personal problems, but also the child's. Parents who themselves can usually remain self-controlled are most likely to help the child learn to discipline himself—a necessary achievement in helping the child face his future.

LEARNING THROUGH PLAY: MATERIALS AND EQUIPMENT

Play is a serious business for all youngsters, providing the best and most constructive outlet for their social and cognitive expansion. It develops the child's spirit of inquiry—which is as natural to him as breathing—unless it is stifled by indifference and censure. To scold him for asking questions, to remain indifferent, or to squelch him for being curious can easily close the door to his mind.

In play, the youngster constantly takes in information through his sensory apparatus, and his incessant moves to discover and explore are endless. He needs to test things out; this is what Myrtle was doing when she threw a record on the ground to "see if it breaks."

The MLD child, usually because of poorer physical coordination, may be a bit clumsier at handling materials and equipment (see Appendix, pages 223–224), and he will need even more space for play than the non-learning disabled; also, probably because he is hampered in receiving and/or sending out messages, he may be slower in taking in the lessons to be learned. Nonetheless, he, too, profits just as much from the concrete objects available in play activity. But the simpler they are, the more they will call on his imagination and initiative. I have seen a child turn from a room full of the most expensive toys, on Christmas Day, to a big heavy carton in the yard. This he played with for many weeks, turning it on every side, as it served his purpose. First he hid in it; then he took his toys and friend inside and played house; later it became a table; and finally, before the snow came, he and his friend were climbing in and out of it. These experiences, in addition, are helping the youngster gain valuable concepts in shape and size, among others— thus aiding in the development of his mental processes.

Knowing the approximate ages that the non-learning disabled child takes in certain ideas can set a guiding pattern for parents of the MLD. It is not uncommon in the regular nursery school to see a boy like four-year-old Jimmy deal with the important concept of size, as he formalizes, "This is a bigger block"; Grace, also age four, in the play yard, is learning about quantity in a relative way by filling her jar with "more" water, until, "but that's too much." Five-year-old Bill is sensing comparison, when he says to his mother, "I've got a bigger cart than Johnny's." Martha, about the same age, was comprehending sequence when she talked about, "First, I'll bathe Abby [her doll], then I'll dress her, then I'll take her on a walk in the carriage."

The MLD need more verbalization from adults: those who understand the ideas that can be gained through the youngster's involvement with simple and uncomplicated materials and equipment can supply valuable guidance, but don't let the deliberate pointers along the way turn into the kind of heavy-handed lectures that so easily destroy a child's initiative and fun. While the child builds with blocks, for example, the parent can make the casual remark, "You're really using a lot of different shapes today. Good for you"; or, as the child paints, "That color blue you're using is like the color blue in your slacks." Sometimes the comment might be turned into a question, but don't demand an answer, and don't allow it to divert or distract the child; for example, "I wonder what you've got on that's like that color blue you're painting with?"

In a meeting with parents once, Mrs. Senden explained to me how she contrived to get into a situation in which her five-year-old Sherry was busy at her various activities. "I'll manage to find an excuse to be around where she is, but as unobtrusively as possible. The other day, when she was at her blocks, I commented, 'That building is taking lots of long and short blocks, isn't it?' Later, when I was reading, her blocks fell over with a great bang. 'What made that?' I asked. 'Too big on top,' she said."

Mrs. Benz got into another track when she asked, "How good is it for our children to be playing alone?" It was a thoughtful question.

Youngsters do need to play with other children for the socialization it affords; this is where the nursery school is an advantage, especially for the MLD who can easily be more isolated. On the other hand, the child who learns to play well alone builds up his own inner resources; this, too, is a plus in social situations.

FREE PLAY AND ITS BENEFITS

The terminology of "free" is used in a comparative sense. In a society of law and order, no one, of course, can be completely free; indeed, the adult who finds himself in the temporary situation of a vacation, without the usual restraints imposed by his customary routine, often finds himself at a loss and wishing for the very irksome things that usually cut down on his "free time."

All children's free play, whether in a school area, or in the family yard, has, hopefully, rules and boundaries, which they know and realize they must abide by. Preschoolers also need the supervision of an adult, who, standing by the sidelines, provides subtle guidance, ready to step in, when the situation calls for it.

Some MLD may be a little below the average in size and build, and in their motor activity; and they may also be less well coordinated. But within a homogeneous grouping, where he is not forced to stand at the fringe because of some inadequacy, or to be unduly aggressive out of frustration, the MLD child profits from the play situation as much as or more than any child.

For parents of youngsters who may seem "wild," it may be a comfort to realize that an outstanding characteristic of the two- to five-year-old is his *constant* activity, as he gains control in the development of his large muscles. These ages are rarely still; they run, jump, climb, and balance. Some of our young adults at PEC, who were overly passive as preschoolers, missed these early growth opportunities through free-play activities because of the limitations a heterogeneous school situation imposed on them, or because of the sterility of the play area.

In almost any activity, young children can have a chance to exercise some physical skills, but free play allows room for the large movements, providing a knowhow that may come in handy later in team games or in individual sports. At the same time, the outdoor space should provide appropriate pieces of equipment and materials; whether building, steering, climbing, or whatever, these functions will enable the child to enter into social functions more easily later on.

In addition, using a cart, big blocks, or other items employs problem solving, as the youngster figures out which piece to use, when, where, how, and for what purpose. This primitive type of thinking takes the child outside of his emotions; it entails an objectivity that is essential to good judgment.

ORGANIZED GAMES

Girl and boy scout leaders have long known that, for the average child, age nine is about the best time for strict teamwork with tight rules. This is equally true for MLD children, who, although they may not be as physically quick or well-coordinated as the non-learning disabled, are ready to play on a team, especially in a homogeneous group. Ages two and three are periods for exploring and trying out—the first steps to mastery of new activities. A person of any age will recognize the steps: the adult, uninitiated in swimming, must learn about appropriate body movement, coordination, and the behavior of water before he can navigate himself; or in tennis, the racquet is handled and skills acquired before the game can be played. Then there are the rules: for the novice—child or adult—they must be strictly adhered to, at first. But as the player grows more certain, comfortable, and relaxed, he feels freer to modify or change them.

Children, learning disabled or not, under about age six, have neither mastered their own motor skills sufficiently, nor are they socially or cognitively well enough developed, to be able to understand or accept being "put out." I don't know how many times I have watched kindergarteners at the game of musical chairs, scrambling wildly to get on the one remaining seat, and seen the last child wilting or crying. Adults should listen to the clues children constantly show, and revise their program accordingly.

All children should begin to learn teamwork through, at first, the loose circle games, often accompanied by the piano or singing: at five, Ring-around-a-rosy and London Bridge are classical examples: at six and seven, games like Duck, Duck Goose, and Red Rover. Between them, and baseball, are the large circle team games of dodge ball, and the like.

In the preschool years, and especially for the MLD child, it is better to encourage him in the fun of playing together and cooperating, instead of pushing him to win. Most MLD usually fold up under competition; and with the major part of their lives full of it, they are more relaxed as they learn that they can get pleasure out of living without being on top.

TRYING ON ROLES

For *all* children, the search for one's identity proceeds in a variety of ways, and over long periods, in a lifetime. At the start, helpless and dependent, and without the use of all of his faculties, the child is aware of other individuals and his environment before he is aware of himself; it's as if he were still functioning through the umbilical cord, so to speak. His own awareness of himself increases as he grows in the ability to detach himself from his surroundings, and as he learns to delay action while he sorts out his thoughts and feelings.

The younger the child, the more he can believe in his own imagination or fantasy. He can raise a stick, point it, and with the accompanying roll of his tongue, shoot and kill. But as he grows older, and is clearer about reality, he will need the Indian gear of clothes and bow and arrow to fill in his imagination, for he no longer believes so completely in his own fantasy.

It is only when the child has enough sense of self, usually late in the third year, that he begins to try on the roles of other people in what is sometimes labeled "dramatic," or "household play." This is when the child tries to put his feet in other people's shoes, in his unconscious efforts to take their place, as he attempts to fathom their life-style; it may also be that he would like their power. At any rate, first he will be acting out the roles of only the figures that are closest to him: mommy, daddy, and maybe the doctor who attends him; by age five and six, he includes neighborhood or regional figures, where the activities are clearly defined: mailman, policeman, fireman, storekeeper, farmer, builder, cowboy, and Indian.

I have never yet seen a young child pretending to be a desk clerk, banker, or lawyer, the activity of such figures probably being too embedded in the job itself, and too subtle for the child to take hold of.

Discarded grown-up clothes that the child can dress in are a delight; the younger the child, the more incongruous the outfit can be. Mommy's pocketbook and a comfort blanket have no trouble harmonizing in the common cause of being the adult. At a moment's notice, too, roles can change, with the baby becoming the mommy, or daddy, the baby.

In our society, children up to about age four or five, unless their innocence has been violated, usually seem indifferent to sexual identity. They probably see it largely as a matter of the clothes that are worn, although this clue must become increasingly complicated in a unisex society. In any case, L. Joseph Stone and Joseph Church of Vassar College report that a four-year-old, when being asked whether the nude baby crawling on the new neighbor's lawn was a boy or girl, said, "I don't know. It is so hard to tell at that age, especially with their clothes off." Be that as it may, the child not only gains some idea of what grown-ups are all about in his real-life play, but he also learns more about who he is, as he takes charge.

THE VALUE OF TRIPS

Trips serve many educational purposes. In addition, especially for the MLD child, they provide natural opportunities to get him outside of the closed confines of his home. But to begin with, excursions to the simplest places prompt the child to sit up and take notice. The results of his observations appear in the child's block building; at first the activity consists of a kind of random trial-and-error exercise, as the youngster explores ways of building with them. For the child who has been out and seen things, though, the shape of the structure takes on real meaning and purpose; his building now becomes a farmhouse with a nearby barn and toy cows coming out of it; or he designs an airport—a space surrounded by a fence made out of blocks. In the field are toy planes lined up for the takeoff.

The younger the child, the easier the excursion should be. For all children under age six, distances should be short, easily traversed, and the destination should be uncrowded. Depending upon one's place of residence, some trips of primary interest for preschoolers are the zoo, airport, seaport, a farm with animals, a building being constructed, and a railroad station. Trips whet the child's curiosity and they are food for thought.

Given that children's attention during these outings can be easily diverted, the teacher or parent should help guide their focus. Only a few things at a time should be concentrated on: several animals at the zoo, the cows being milked, the airplanes coming in and taking off, the movement of the derrick at a construction site. Children are fascinated by movement. Still, there is no harm in displaying one's pleasure over flowers or shrubs, or other beautiful things in the landscape en route to the destination. Learning disabled or not, too many individuals seem to be in the perpetual state of the two-year-old for whom things "just are"; one might say that all good teaching is a matter of "making the obvious evident."

GIVING AND FOLLOWING DIRECTIONS

Anyone who has been lost may realize how few people know how to give directions, and probably a great number don't know how to follow them either, even when they are good. For many MLD, who have a hard time with location, being on the receiving end is a greater disadvantage; for, unless the directions are explicit, given one at a time, and in words that have a clear and undisguised meaning, they grope in bewilderment.

The younger the child, the greater the difficulty, as Mrs. Draik demonstrated, in recounting her experience one day at a school meeting. She told her son, almost six, to "go upstairs and get your heavy gloves and bring them down with my pocketbook." Sometime later Gregg descended the stairs with the wrong gloves and no pocketbook.

"These aren't your heavy gloves, Gregg." Mrs. Draik was irritated. "And where is my pocketbook?"

"Well, at school the kids call these my 'hairy' gloves," was Gregg's reply, with no mention of the second item.

Gregg had obviously confused "hairy" with "heavy"; he needed to be told to "go upstairs and get your brown gloves with the fur lining." Probably he forgot the pocketbook, or, perhaps he had no idea where it was; in any case, after bringing the gloves down, Mrs. Draik's second request should have given a clear description of the pocketbook and exactly where it was located.

There are steps that can help the MLD child to be more comfortable with directions and locating things, and the earlier they are taken, the better, although this game may have to wait until the child is in the primary grades. If a beginning can be made at the end of the kindergarten year, however, go ahead, keeping in mind, though, that the average second and third grader finds mapping very difficult.

Begin with purchasing—if you can build it so much the better—a dollhouse, with at least four rooms, the roof of which comes off. It should be conventionally furnished. Also, have at your side a small figure of a doll and a dog or a cat, or all three figures. The house will delight young children, and games in it will be fun.

With the roof off, and looking down on the rooms, have the child name every piece of furniture, the windows and doors, and the rooms they are in. Then contrive a series of games through which the youngster will identify each object and its location. "I see a bed. What room is it in?" "What room is the lamp in?" Then put one of the figures on a chair. "Where is the doll?" "What room is it in?"

Next, proceed to the child's own movement: "Come in the front door, and with your finger show me just how you will find the doll." Have the child name every step of the way, as he moves from one room to the other. Gradually add new dimensions: "You're in the kitchen, it's raining and the window in the bedroom has to be closed. Where do you go to do it? How?"

Another step is to have the child close his eyes and work from memory. "The cat is on the table. What room is it in?" "You're in the bedroom and you hear someone at the kitchen door. How do you get there from the bedroom?"

Many of our young MLD adults do not give enough attention to the details of their surroundings, nor are they conscious enough of the directions in which they move. If, as youngsters, they have some exercises in the game of "house play," or anything similar to it, they will be better off later on.

NUMBER READINESS

Pouring knowledge into any child's mind, and rote learning, may give some exercise to the memory without necessarily involving the thought process. A five-year-old, who runs up the scale from one to one hundred, knows the words without comprehending the meaning: counting numbers is very different from distinguishing between them.

Before age two or later, the non-learning disabled

child will try to fit very big things into small ones; around this age, too, he may count four trucks, but say two when asked how many. But by the time he goes to the first grade, especially if he has been to nursery school, through socializing and play experiences, he learns to understand something about the relativity of light, heavy, short, tall, small, big, and so on. He also measures things against each other: two of these blocks make one of those; this block will fit into that space. Then, gradually, he is learning about morning, afternoon, before, after, now, soon, later, and so on. The days and months are becoming familiar, and he becomes aware of the succession of the four seasons, as well as the recurrence of holidays. All of these concepts are indigenous to number.

Kindergarteners, who are not drilled, will count things, usually up to about five, but when it comes to breezing up the ladder of digits, their confusions emerge as they must identify the number with the thing it stands for. Typical of this was the child I recently watched counting; touching each classmate—a good idea—she proceeded: 1, 2, 3, 4, 7, 8, 11, 13, 14, 17, 21, 23. About this age, the child rarely has any idea that eight ones are less than nine, or that nine ones are more than eight. As for the ideas that deal with measurement, or value of any kind, these are usually well beyond his cognitive powers; and with his lack of a sense of constancy, anything formal in the way of "relative to," is more than he can handle.

The MLD will probably be slower in number comprehension than the average child, and he will need much patience and help as he approaches the ideas that concern quantity. Exposure to these concepts, through direct experiences, are essential to his eventual understanding of the symbols themselves, and to the formal operations in which they are engaged.

Few adults are aware of the process of, and the need for, gradualism in learning. In number readiness this can take place for any child, including the MLD, as he builds with blocks and sees that he needs "one more," or has "too many," or that the last block on top made his building fall over.

Parents and teachers of the MLD should verbalize these concepts as the occasion arises: "Put your shoes on *first*." "You may take *two* cookies." "This is the *last* day of school." "Put *one* spoon in front of each chair." "Let's put *two* cups of water in the Jell-O." "The soup needs a *little* salt." "You have a *lot* of marbles."

Mathematical experience with size, order, and amount, no matter what man works at, or where he lives, are the characteristics of experiences with quantity. The MLD's exercises with these notions will greatly help him in his other arithmetical operations.

USING THE ENVIRONMENT

The non-learning disabled child's explorations from his earliest days provide fuel for his mental development. At first his doings are tied up with his physical growth, and his relationship with others; but as he comes to realize that facts are valuable links in the chain of his understanding, and that his understanding enables him to master his environment, he seeks facts for themselves.

In teaching a class of any first graders, it is usually easy to tell the children who have been exposed to a variety of experiences, for they are often more curious, observant, and questioning—qualities essential to thinking.

The environment provides multifarious ways to help the child's cognitive development, be he a non-learning disabled child or an MLD. The importance of sensory intake is indisputable; for the MLD, the early opportunities to discriminate using his sensory apparatus, as he learns to recognize differences, similarities, and relationships, is an educational advantage. Talking about what he perceives is also essential for the MLD child. Whether young or old, whatever anyone thinks remains formless in his mind until he translates it into symbols —numbers, pictures, or the like. Symbolization is essential to thinking.

Listening and watching children, one can realize how easily they live with inconsistencies and contradictions. Mr. Hart and his three-and-a-half-year-old son, Dirk, examined some pebbles they were collecting on the beach. Mr. Hart was careful to call attention to the different shapes and colors.

Shortly afterward, Dirk began to play with a neighbor's child. "First the pebbles were candy," Mr. Hart said. "Then they pretended that they were orange juice and 'we've got to drink it.' But you knew that they knew they were pretending, because they didn't attempt to chew or drink the pebbles."

By the age of seven or eight, or earlier, depending on the child, the MLD can become aware of classification. Mrs. Wane had that in mind when she took her daughter Kim on their many walks.

On this one they collected a bell, some dried leaves, an old whistle that Mrs. Wane washed off, pebbles, twigs, stones, and rocks.

On a rainy day, Mrs. Wane got down three empty shoe boxes, saying. "Let's tidy up these things, Kim, so you can find the whistle or bell, or anything you want to play with."

Spreading the pile on the kitchen table, Kim's mother asked, "What should we put in the first box?"

"These." Kim picked up the pebbles.

"OK. What next?"

Kim picked up the whistle and tentatively put it in the second box.

"Good, Kim. Now what?"

"Could the bell go in this one?" Kim pointed to the third box.

"It could, sure. But it would fit something in one of the other boxes."

Kim looked blank. "What makes a noise, Kim?"

"The bell?" Shaking it.

"What else makes a sound?"

"The whistle?"

"So?"

Kim delightedly put the whistle and bell together.

"Now?"

Kim, with more assurance, put the leaves in the third box.

"Where do you think the twigs should go?"

"With the pebbles?"

"Why?"

"They're rough, too?"

"Yes, Kim, but they come off a tree. What do you have in a box that also comes off a tree?"

Kim put the twigs with the leaves. Then she picked up the stones and rocks. "With the pebbles?" she asked.

"Great!" Mrs. Wane was excited now. "Why?"

"They're all hard and white!" The youngster was triumphant.

"They're not all exactly white, Kim, but they *are* all hard. You've done a good job." Mrs. Wane gave Kim a hug.

On a daily basis, adults can be more casual in the points they want to make. "It's the wind; it's so strong that it's hard to walk against it"; or, "The boiling water makes the steam come out of the spout"; or, "The melting snow makes all of the puddles"; or, "See how the rope is pulling the man up so he can reach the windows?" If appropriate, and the comment can be turned into a question to which the child appears to be receptive, turn it into, "What is pulling the man up to the windows?"

Whatever the approach, the MLD who is helped to look at what he is seeing will do better thinking.

THE VALUE OF PLANTS AND ANIMALS

In caring for plants and animals, the MLD child can learn a positive attitude toward life. This turns on a sense of responsibility for live things besides the child himself. It also includes facing the reality of death; the gradual realization that all life must die makes it more precious. In this day of easy disposal, that is no small matter.

As far as plants go, young children can enjoy the experience of sowing seeds, watching for their growth—if the plants chosen don't take too long to sprout—and caring for the vegetation. This activity can become a worthwhile and enjoyable hobby later on.

Animals, of course, are easiest for the child to identify with: creatures, who, like themselves, need food and water and to be cleaned, who wilt and get tired, and need protection. Keep in mind, though, that the able child, until he is about fourteen, and the MLD possibly later, is not ready for *complete* responsibility of the animal. That is something best arrived at by the gradual approach, beginning with fetching food and helping to brush fur. These little steps can begin by first grade. Whatever the methods, the adult's attitude toward these growing things will have the greatest influence. It is incongruous and confusing to have plants and animals in the home if you find them a burden and a nuisance.

The death, especially of a beloved pet, prepares the child for the pain he may have to face later with the loss of a close member of the family. The expression of grief, through tears and questions, is a sign of health; one cannot prevent suffering, but one can comfort the sufferer. Often the child's questions about death are disconcerting because the grown-up to whom they are posed invests them with adult meaning. Still, the child's inquiries should be answered simply and in accordance with the parents' own philosophy and religion: "His soul was taken to heaven"; or, "God took him away"; or, "Flowers die, animals die, people die; no one lives forever."

To tell the child that the deceased went to sleep can be frightening, since it makes sleep synonymous with death; even some adults have a hard time separating the difference. It is false comfort, too, to indicate that the deceased will come back again, since that creates an unreal anticipation, ending in a kind of mistrust. In the same vein, to tell a child not to cry because you will go out and buy him another animal misplaces a healthy emotion. Love cannot be replaced by cash.

In this connection, I recall the beautiful manner in which a father helped his young six-year-old son when his Scottish terrier died. If nothing else, it added some thought to the child's grief.

Placing his arm comfortingly around the boy's shoulders, Mr. Briggs said gently and kindly, "That's life, Glenn; all things must die."

"But I don't want it that way," Glenn sobbed.

"Nobody does," his father said. "But we love and enjoy life while we have it, and your good feelings about Scotty will help you to love another living animal."

READING READINESS

For the MLD, as well as for the non-learning disabled, listening to language, and communicating, are first steps to talking and reading. Parents can devise a number of ways to help the youngster in the process, but first a few helpful pointers.

All preschoolers' use of language and understanding of words are grasped in terms of ability, age, and experience; but the way the child speaks, and his interest and desire to express himself, will largely depend on his home environment, to begin with, and later, the schools he attends.

Most human beings need to be engaged in the functions of work, study, and socializing, to spark the mental processes of thinking; but unless thoughts are transcribed into some kind of verbal or written symbols, they remain pieces of dough on the mind.

Children's language facility is encouraged not only through listening and reading, but through all kinds of experiences, many of which are recounted throughout this text; activities are fuel to language expression.

But learning to read is a lifetime job. The genuine reader continues to expand and deepen his vocabulary of words and meanings, and to refine his skills, as long as he is able.

Reading developed late in the history of man; the process is not inherent to the child's development, but the necessity arises from his culture; indeed, there are still some cultures left that do not require reading, and even in our own, a child born a few generations ago could have managed without it.

Children's success in reading is undoubtedly tied up with the satisfaction they get out of it. Many of the Marginally Learning Disabled's difficulties in abstracting and integrating complex ideas discourage his desire, yet with the proper encouragement and help, he can usually do well enough to manage the books he needs to read; and some can read for enjoyment alone, especially with the increase in appropriate storybooks for this population.

Labels and signs are one good way to start all preschoolers off: "John's closet," "John's shelf," "John's hanger," as well as the labels in his clothes; also the signs on boxes containing the things he uses: puzzles, crayons, brushes, pencils, scissors, marbles, blocks, and the like. Then there are the picture books that the child enjoys looking at alone, or with an adult who can read the captions that go with them or elicit the child's comments.

Fitting together simple puzzles, and matching picture games, sharpen the young child's eye for different and similar shapes, colors, and patterns, a discrimination necessary in reading. Hearing stories, whether out of books, or simply recounted factual tales, may also whet his desire to conquer the written symbol. And, as already indicated, another way is to encourage him to tell his own story as you write it down.

Books for young children fall into two broad categories, known as the "here and now," and fantasy, or make-believe; many stories combine the two elements. Understanding how the child thinks will help in the selection of his books.

In the preschooler's thinking, magic is very active. The three-and-a-half-year-old who can turn pebbles into orange juice has the idea that, like the pilot who can keep the plane in the sky, or daddy who can make the car move, he can will things to happen.

The six-year-old who asked, "Does Blacky know he is a dog?" is reflecting his growing consciousness of who *he* is and what is what, more than younger children do. A good illustration is the group of four-year-olds who became terrified when their mothers paraded into the nursery school in Halloween costumes. The children who did not cry at first caught the fear very quickly from those who did, and all continued to cry after their mothers took their costumes off. Some of the frightened children had heard their mothers discuss the plan beforehand; what the parents did not realize is that the child's fantasy can quickly overwhelm his sense of reality—as it can with many adults in certain situations. The children were not so certain that people cannot turn into hobgoblins and witches.

Some knowledge of children gives us clues to their thinking and the best kind of choices. Children under age six are far better off with stories of their real world; tales about other children, other families, animals, country or city life, trains, dolls, boats, airplanes, the fireman and the policeman, provide excitement enough, as well as adding lots of new and valuable information, if the stories are well done and appropriate.

As for the child's imagination, he has plenty of that, without the kinds of grisly fantasy presently cropping up in some of the TV shows, movies, and storybooks. By age five, fantasy can be woven nicely into the here-and-now stories; after all, by that time, most children know that witches really do not exist, although, like some adults, they may continue secretly to believe otherwise.

Fairy tales, of the Grimm and Andersen variety, can well wait until the child is seven. A librarian friend of mine recently told me that they are still most popular with children of the middle years, despite the glut of

Superman and way-out epics, in which human behavior is distorted and twisted.

Stories of violence and morbidity should always be avoided; there is enough for the child to see in everyday life, despite the best parental guidance.

4

As the MLD Child
Grows Older

FACING LIFE

Increasingly, as he gets older, probably because he feels
that he cannot learn, the MLD individual usually tends
to hide his head in the sand more than the average person. It is possible that not looking around him very
closely makes him more fearful, too. For most MLD,
many of life's more subtle events—like the turn of the
seasons—go on with hardly any sense of wonder on their
part. Teaching the MLD, then, is partially the business
of illuminating the features on the face of life; the MLD
need to be taught how to observe and examine.

In helping these individuals to grapple with their problems, we are occasionally asked if concentration on their
deficits may not be detrimental to their self-esteem. The
question reflects the wrong slant: first, the student recognizes that we work from his strengths, meanwhile di-
minishing his weaknesses; and, second, the learning-
handicapped person feels no less normal facing his deficits than in hiding them; if anything, the relief felt in

trying to cope with his problems joins him more closely to the human race. For all of us, there is nothing more debilitating than trying to hide difficulties that darken our lives; in fact, when the energy to cover them up is redirected to the solution of our problems, life takes on fresh vigor and strength.

EXPANDING EXPERIENCES

Older children who have left block play behind profitably continue some of the same activities as the younger child, but an expanding intellect changes the student's purposes and goals: art and shop and home economics will take on a very different look, as will the things they collect.

The middle schooler can also engage in activities of a more abstract nature, although these must be tied to the concrete as much as possible. (The Schneider Science Series is the best aid to adults who teach the Marginally Learning Disabled that I know.) The study of electricity, for a fourteen-year-old group, for example, might grow out of wiring a dollhouse that has been constructed in shop. Other interests can be guided in the exploration of plant, animal, marine, farm, and city life; lumbering; exploration of the magnet and compass; a study of rocks and minerals; experimenting with a magnifying lens, microscope, and binoculars; and the study of weather, using the thermometer. The geographical location should, of course, influence the emphasis.

DIRECTION AND SPACE

The child, MLD or not, has different ideas about space and travel from the adult's, and it takes him a few years to clarify them. Stone and Church, in their excellent text on the child's development, *Childhood and Adolescence*,* present the stages in the development of his spatial concepts. Since many MLD children have a very difficult time dealing with direction and space, the authors' presentation should be of great interest to adults who care for or teach MLD individuals. For our purposes here, I offer an abridgment of their account.

Although the individual usually operates on several different levels at the same time, the authors enumerate five steps, the first being *action space*, which takes in the areas within which the youngster moves, as well as the locations to which he anchors his body; *body space* includes his sense of distance and direction, as they relate to his own body; and in *object space*, he is able to take in direction and distance through objects in reference to each other.

The last two stages, usually interdependent, are, briefly, *map space*, as it amplifies and integrates concrete spatial experiences. These experiences are translated into "mental maps," that depend on "some system of co-ordinates or cardinal directions," covering such small spaces as rooms to such large geographical regions as nations; the final stage, *abstract space*, is connected with the ability to deal with navigational and astronomical

* *Childhood and Adolescence* (New York: Random House, 1957), pp. 185–86.

problems and it is rarely within the young child's scope of understanding.

Stone and Church go on to show the preschooler as he experiences the stages preceding map or schematized abstract space—stages almost always beyond the young child's ken. Conquering action space, the familiar terrain in which he moves, the preschooler explores body space, as it relates to his corporeal self; now he begins to familiarize himself with such directions as up and down, next to, near and far, in front of, and behind—*always* in relationship to himself. Those familiar with the child's behavior know that it will be a while longer before he can discriminate between left and right, or with directions that go beyond his own personal perception.

One can see how bound the child is to the pattern of his actions, too, in the way he may balk at taking a detour from the route on which he is usually taken. In an old school building, full of mazes and flights of stairs, three-and-a-half-year-old Lily obstinately refused to go up an unfamiliar flight to her classroom, with the assistant teacher, whom she knew well.

As Stone and Church point out, as the child gets older, he gradually forms a unified idea of the spatial regions he knows, even being able to think about something "around the corner," and to take detours. The authors speculate that the reason the preschooler does not yet play hide-and-seek is that he cannot think of himself and objects as part of a large, integrated spatial scheme; but within his small framework, brief hiding games and chasing are a delight to his heart.

It is not unusual for MLD young adults to have a difficult time locating themselves in relationship to direction and space, if they have not had help in this area as they grew up. One of our poignant moments at PEC was in hearing twenty-year-old Vera, a very attractive, able second-year student, boast to her friends, "Hey, guess what? I can get from my house to my school all alone now, without any trouble!"

In laterality, the majority know their left and right on themselves, but some have difficulty figuring it out on someone else facing them. This is a disadvantage in their fieldwork, when, as teacher aides, they try to help the child put on his shoes. Much has been written on the subject, with practical suggestions to help the MLD. A good idea is to have the MLD youngster wear a ring on one hand, marking it as left or right, whichever the case may be; another method is to have him study himself in the mirror, where he can figure out that left and right on the figure that stands opposite to him is a reversal of his own left and right.

In using the suggestions below, make the procedure a fun game, and proceed slowly with the MLD, and with *great* patience, remembering that the average third and fourth graders find regular map reading difficult. Gradual steps, though, always help; depending on the MLD child, some may be ready for these games at age seven or eight or possibly earlier.

Begin with the dollhouse game discussed in chapter 3. Once the child can comfortably locate the rooms, windows, and doors, identify the objects, accurately relate them to the right rooms, and properly follow the routes, move on to the next step.

Have a photograph of the house made from above, with the roof off, then play the game without the doll and animal figures, having the child go through the same kind of exercises of following routes on the two-dimensional representation.

Next, on a sheet of paper the dimension of the house, draw the exact floor plan. As in an architectural design, mark out the windows and doors. Designate the furniture, lamps, and other objects by circles, squares, rectangles, or whatever shapes represent them most clearly.

Now have the child read this map, identifying and locating all of the room spaces and objects and managing his routes to and from them.

Another helpful device is through the use of a very simply drawn "concrete" map of the child's room, or the space he usually frequents. Involving your child in the venture, lay a large sheet of heavy paper on the floor, almost large enough to cover it if possible. On the sheet, glue or staple pieces of toy furniture that represent the pieces in the room—bed, table, or whatever, labeling each article. Then, devise a search procedure with the youngster, hiding an object, perhaps a ball, near the real furniture in the room. By using the miniature replicas on the paper map, point to one, perhaps the dresser, that represents the place next to which you hid the ball. Tell the child, "The ball is under the dresser," or, "next to it," or, "on top of it," whichever the case may be. If the child is able to manage "left" and "right," incorporate those into the directions. Once the child catches on to this, or to any of the other preceding games, for that matter, reverse roles, and have him hide the ball, directing you. After he has mastered this space, move into another room, using the same procedures.

When the "concrete" map has been played out, take the miniature furniture off it, and play the game using the labels. If there are a few days between the game, and if it is possible, hang the map on a wall for the child to see it from a different vantage point. Don't leave it up endlessly, though, after interest has waned. Stale exhibits discourage the child from looking, as anyone knows who has observed in some classrooms.

From the mapping of his home, walk with the child into his neighborhood; choose several blocks he travels over most frequently and with which he is most familiar. On a large but manageable sheet of paper, designate the landmarks he knows, drawing and clearly labeling them:

a space of green for a park, a rectangle or other appropriate shapes for the school, and so on. As you move along the sidewalk, have the child point to the places on the map as you pass them; also have him tell you what comes next by looking at the map. Once he knows the route, have him tell it to you at home, from memory. Finally, draw a map on which only the routes themselves are drawn, in clear, dark lines, with large dots or circles representing the buildings and other landmarks he knows. Needless to say, all of these games are useful for classroom teachers, too.

Another good activity for both home and school is the large table map; my middle graders loved creating one, and they learned a lot as they worked on it. Using a big sheet of metal or wood, or any appropriate material for the base, begin, again, mapping out the area the child knows best—his home surroundings. Involve him in the creation, from the beginning, by taking the child outside to look over the territory; together decide what things should be on the table map. Cover the foundation with soil, grass, or whatever pictures the scene, then place the house, possibly made out of cardboard or any other appropriate material, on it, and have the child help you to locate it. For the rest of the map, let the child, with your guidance when necessary, use his imagination. My students have used soil for hills, covering them with grass, or salt for snow in the winter; some have painted in streams, lakes, or a pool, or used aluminum foil, and, in one instance, real glass; twigs were used for trees, trimmed with bits of green muslin, for leaves, and so on. Besides helping the child to manage space and direction, this project offers excellent opportunities for using ingenuity in choosing and converting materials, as well as developing skills in handwork.

Another directional aid is to have the child fetch things within the home or familiar nearby places. Giving very explicit directions, ask the child to "Please get the watering can. It is in the basement, next to the sink"; or, "It is in the garage in the corner, next to the window."

A self-service market is another good situation for exploring, as any shopper knows, providing you can take your child when it is not crowded, and when you have plenty of time. Figure out what the child can get beforehand, telling him you need his help. Show him the article at home that he is to find in the store, helping him write the name down, so that he can refer to it in the shop if he needs to.

Begin with having him fetch one article, at first, and something that is easy to find. Facing the proper direction with him, tell the youngster, pointing, that "The quart of milk is at the back of the store, in that corner"; or, "The sugar is two aisles over there [pointing], on the bottom shelf." When the child cannot find the article, go with him, show him where it is, then, both returning to your place of origin, let him fetch it by himself, immediately afterward.

If you have the time and patience, and there can be a fun quality to these experiences, your child will be able to get around on his own long before our twenty-year-old PEC student, Vera, did.

CHORES

Occasionally we get a PEC young adult who resents helping with the chores in his fieldwork placement. The parents of such children often say, "He's lazy," or, "He never helps at home either," or, "I can't stand it when he helps; he's slow, and he never does anything right."

If the MLD youngster has been trained early and gradually, he gains a valuable sense of satisfaction through active participation, the social contact it brings, and in being useful and needed, feelings he desperately needs. But in the beginning, the chores must fit the child's abilities and he will need help: picking up his toys or his clothes and handing them to you while you put them away; or carrying his own dishes to the kitchen; or, as he grows older, taking the garbage out, picking leaves off the lawn, making his own bed—these are natural and simple ways to help the child feel a responsible part of the household that can become a way of life for him. I can still recall Mrs. Elwer's telling me: "When Jane was little I didn't think it was fair to ask her. Now when she's eighteen and I ask her, she says, 'I don't know how to do that,' or, 'Where's John? Why ask me all of a sudden?' "

Most MLD need more patience, more good humor, and more praise than the non-disabled learner. Real effort put into a job, although only half well done, is a healthy forward step.

It is better to let a six-year-old put his toys away, however long it takes him, than habitually to grab the situation out of his hands and do it for him. But no parent needs to worry about an occasional show of impatience, for it is the everyday way of life that counts most in the child's upbringing.

Deserved praise and encouragement, and fitting your standards to the child's abilities, bring the best deposit. Mrs. Dalson quoted her son, age eleven, as saying, "I can never please you, so why try?" Tears came to her eyes as she added, "You know, he's right."

"Maybe he is," I responded, "but the fact that he could tell you that so clearly, and that you understand why he feels that way, already begins to improve the situation."

About a year later, when I ran into Mrs. Dalson, she eagerly let me know that things were better between her and her son, "but not perfect," she put in.

"They wouldn't be perfect with a son who didn't have a learning handicap," was my reply.

"I guess just trying to be a good parent is hard."

It's fruitful to try, I thought to myself. Fruit mellows the tree.

TRIPS

As I mentioned earlier, parents of MLD children should be sure to plan ways for them to take trips outside of the home as soon as possible. However, as they grow older, the excursion can be farther away and more complicated in substance; still, don't be afraid of repeating a trip that the child went on when he was younger, if it is rich in possibilities; the eight-year-old sees more and different things now in a visit to the farm, harbor, or zoo than when he was a child of five, and his pleasure is just as great.

Be specific about what the child will see, thus focusing his attention, and helping his understanding. When Mrs. Tonson told her son Jackson, age six, "We're going to the harbor to see the *Queen Mary*," he asked, "Will she wear a diamond crown?"

At a parents' meeting where a discussion of trips was going on, one parent was quick to advise Mrs. Tonson: "You should tell Jackson that he is being taken to a place on the water. Large ships come and go from there; it is called a 'harbor.' There will be a very big ship to visit called the *Queen Mary*."

Another parent, Mrs. Wessler, shared her seven-year-old Mary's confusion with us and how she set it straight: "I began with, 'We are going to the Sweet Fern to see some animals.' I simply took it for granted that she knows what that is. Well, she didn't."

"Monkeys and tigers!" she exclaimed.

"I then carefully explained that we were going to the Sweet Fern Dairy Farm where there are cows, pigs, and chickens. It was a great trip. The next day, we found some pictures of the animals we had seen, cut them out, and tacked them up on her bulletin board. She got a lot out of that trip, besides traveling away from home."

In taking her seven-and-a-half-year-old Bart on longer trips, Mrs. Parkman told the parents: "I found it easier for both of us when I am very specific. I tell him, 'We will go there right after lunch. It's about as long a trip as when we go to Pound Beach.' If I tell him that we are going on a longer trip, he keeps asking, 'How much longer is it?' or, 'What's a little farther away?' It also helps us both a lot if I can give him some idea of the way we will go: 'Past Jan's house, past Star's fruit stand,' and so on. Then he uses up the time looking for and identifying places instead of nagging me and being so restless."

As the MLD reaches his teens, it is hoped that his school will involve him in outside excursions. They should grow out of his interests and studies, and he should be involved in the planning, including the transportation rules, if an entire class is involved. Time during the visit should be allowed for the student's questions; in addition, there needs to be some discussion after the excursion to help integrate the information.

Subjects of a more complicated nature might include trips to an outdoor food market, a processing plant, a fish hatchery, a weather station, and a lumber camp; museums and historical sites can be profitable, too, if they are tied to famous and interesting historical figures. Whatever excursion is undertaken, it needs some thoughtful planning and preparation ahead, if it is to be profitable and enjoyable.

CROSSING
THE HOME BOUNDARY LINE
ALONE

Many PEC young adults find it very difficult to travel independently and find their own way. Invariably, every year, we have students who are afraid to move out on their own, or who cannot find their way over a route that they constantly traverse.

Working with the MLD, we find that the main difficulty of most of them is their lack of independent experience; having been chauffeured all their lives from place to place by caring, anxious parents, they are over-protected and more fearful than they would otherwise be.

Some MLD can be taken advantage of very easily, and it does take courage to let them go long distances alone; yet reasonable chances must be taken if they are not to become crippled human beings. But even at that, we are delighted to see how quickly most of the PEC students catch on, despite a poor sense of direction, and how thrilled they are once they can steer themselves; in fact, by the time of graduation, the majority of those not from New York—a city to which many parents are originally afraid to send them—want to remain. As the parents come to realize, New York is as safe as any other large metropolis, and the many advantages it offers PEC students—in the ease with which they can get around without a car, and the activities at their disposal—make it an advantageous place to stay.

As already specified, helping the MLD to manage in

space and direction should begin as early as possible. After the child has been out of the home with adults, *walking*, and by car, and when he can communicate easily, various ways should be found to get him to go on nearby errands. Mrs. Stafferd said she began preparing her seven-year-old Mabel by taking her on walks to neighbors, who lived in close proximity. "I would ask her, 'Where do we turn now? Which way do we turn? Is it on this side of the street or the other side? Run ahead and show me where Mrs. Long lives.' "

"Mabel would be so pleased to be asked," she went on, "that she got so that she would volunteer the information ahead of time. And it sure got her ready for the errands that I sent her on when she was old enough to go alone."

Mrs. Well told the parents' group that she began her son on errands at age eight and a half. "I would walk or drive to a store, give him the exact change, and wait outside while he went in to make the purchase of a quart of milk, or some grocery item that he knew well. He loved the responsibility."

Dolly Eames, about eight, got started a little differently. "We were lucky," her mother explained, "in having my husband's sister several doors down the block. We worked it out so that she would call up Dolly and ask her to come over and get some cake she had baked to bring to me, or I would have Dolly take her something I wanted to send. Then we got several neighbors in on the plan, even the Jackses *across* the street. Dolly learned to obey the lights meticulously in getting over, as I knew from watching her from behind the curtains—with my heart in my mouth, at first."

Whether residing in the country, town, or city, if you want to be certain your child won't be handicapped in traveling alone as an adult, take some deliberate measures in training him to move away from home under his own steam by the time he is in the first grade; do remember, though, that the process should be slow and gradual.

SOCIALIZATION

One of the most abiding problems of many of the MLD is their lifetime feelings of isolation and loneliness. By the age of eighteen, when they have opportunities to join in group activities, as our young PEC adults do, their immaturity, as the result of their lack of social experience, often makes it impossible for them to function successfully.

If the MLD schooling is within a homogeneous setting, their chances for having at least one friend in the earlier grades are much better. But before any real socializing can take place, the child needs the experience of learning how to play reasonably well by himself, for short periods of time, at various activities; also, he will need to have learned how to discipline himself within his own family group, realizing what it means to share and cooperate.

Normally, friendships grow out of the casual, side-by-side play of the three-year-old to the shifting group play of the kindergartener, to having friends in the first or second grade.

The early primary years, six to eight, begin the "gang age" that flowers at about ten and eleven. During this period, children's play is often organized into large-group games, held together with a set pattern of behavior or a kind of ritual; eeny, meeny, miney, mo, hide-and-seek, marbles, red rover, giant steps, and hopscotch are good examples.

Keeping and telling secrets, now that the child can

keep his thoughts to himself, is noticeably in the foreground, as well as the tendency to be a copycat. Male and female groups, at least in our present culture, tend to play separately, as the children get nearer the third grade, and scapegoats are common; the children also begin to measure their skills against each other.

Clubs are most fitting about age nine. If there is no social group available to your MLD child by the time he is in the fifth grade, help to organize one through your school, religious group, or the Association for the Learning Disabled. The MLD's social development, at best, has its ups and downs, and parental support and encouragement are needed in the process. Your child's ability to connect with and have some friends will connect him with life itself.

THE MEANING BEHIND SYMBOLS

A symbol, such as a word or a number, spoken or written, is a tangible representation of any one of a number of concrete things. It can be "1" or "2," or "one" or "two," meaning the number of candies, stones, or pencils; the word "dog" stands for a certain animal; rose means a particular flower. One way the MLD copes with his difficulties in shaping the ideas related to the symbols is to memorize them. All of us know in what desperation we have consciously resorted to memorizing number combinations, or a string of words, without comprehending the meaning that lies behind them. This is not to deride the need for, and the use of, memory in learning, but memorization without understanding freezes thinking.

Occasionally, our judgment of a child's ability is

thrown off as a result of his feats of memory. Some musician friends of mine were ecstatic because their child, Hans, age two and a quarter, seemed suddenly to read spontaneously the names of the composers on the turntable records that the parents constantly played; but they soon discovered this did not mean that Hans could read. At the same time, what they did not realize was that his memorization of the shapes of the names, and identifying them with the music, displayed a valuable skill in the discrimination of form, and an association with meaning, that would come in handy later on.

In many of the university classes that I taught, the students were teachers; several who instructed kindergarten children, age five, claimed that some of their children understood the numbers up to twenty or more because they could count to them. I suggested that they take twenty objects—cookies or candies, and twenty pennies, and show the equivalency of one to one, and the sum total. The teachers reported that the children were greatly confused; among the reasons were that the twenty cookies or candies made a longer line than the twenty pennies, and that they were larger.

Another student, a teacher of second graders, age seven, reported that she was sure her children understood the fraction "one-half," that they knew "by heart" that two halves equal one whole, and that she had carefully used concrete objects to teach this principle. But after our class discussions, and pursuing the subject further, she found that the children were thrown off when they were presented with halves of different sizes and shapes—a confusion to be expected in the thinking of sevens.

The point is that, although these first gradual steps in learning are essentials, they hardly reflect a *complete* grasp of the proposition. In the case of number, there is a long distance between the concept, or understanding, and the ability to count or name a figure.

Aside from that, the erroneous concepts one keeps in one's head, as one grows older, are legion. Once my fifth grader, Linda, age ten, pointing to the ceiling, explained to the class that north is always up, that east is on the right, and west in on the left; at another time, in that same grade, Tom asked, "But doesn't water have to run down *south?* How can it run up *north?*" These children had always been taught geography by a flat map hung on the wall in front of the classroom.

Another time, taking a fourth grade to a camp, when it included crossing a state line, Geraldine asked, *"Where is the boundary line?"* A few of the children also expressed surprise that the country looked the same although we were in a different state.

Adults, too, have faulty concepts, or great gaps in knowledge. Some of my university students found it difficult to see how a mountain and a lake are related (they are both geographical features), although they readily saw the differences. Like the children who need more than a wall map to take in directions and the meaning of a boundary line, their teachers had shortchanged them. Unfortunately, too few educators are aware of such gaps and confusions.

VERBAL COMMUNICATION

I don't know how many times I have been in family gatherings where the MLD child sits like a bump on a log, all kinds of conversation going on about his head, while he is completely overlooked. Chances are he will listen to gossip about people he is acquainted with, or anything dramatic in nature—marriages, birth, death, divorces, and the like—but discussions concerning more abstract things—politics, the state of economy, and business affairs—will go in one ear and out the other.

MLD or not, meaningful communication is more likely to grow out—and not on top—of interests. For the MLD this involves appropriate activities, plus, of course, the necessary verbal skills. Story dictation, suggested above, can profitably continue as a family game throughout the child's elementary-school years, but with the various members of the family participating. The child might begin the tale, and the others continue it, the length depending on the child's inclination. For the primary ages, at least, one of the parents can record the story, with the child copying it later. This same procedure can be carried out as a class endeavor, as well.

The preschooler's interests (seen in the last chapter) in collections, taking trips, having an animal, playing games, and by nine or ten, being part of a club, will, hopefully, grow into full-blown benefits for him when he is a teenager and adult.

At that later period, other interests will be added, such as sports, music, and movies. One family, the Healds, whose fourteen-year-old son, Roscoe, took hold of their interest in ecology, was put in charge of the weekly cleanup of the roadsides in the neighborhood. All of this business, beginning early, provides meat for the MLD's conversation.

Guidelines along the way, for parents and teachers, are more easily realized if there is some awareness of the verbal development of the non-learning disabled child. To begin with, verbal communication can include a world of substance: talking, and then the important distance to conversing, is a step that all young children find difficult, MLD or otherwise. Conversation is different from talking per se; it includes planning, discussing, reporting, self-expression, sharing, evaluating, solving problems, and creative expression. Many MLD parents throw up their hands at this list of accomplishments until they realize that a number of them mesh together in the verbal expression of a single idea. At any rate, as food is essential for the body, so is the ability to communicate essential for the growth of intelligence.

Effective speaking is impossible without listening. In the early years of the child's life he does little conscious listening, unless the subject is directly concerned with himself—a period many adults have not grown out of! Also, he is easily distracted, with his first listening being partial, while he waits to insert his own idea. This can be seen in the three-year-old's play: Jane, filling her pail with sand, says, "My mommy is getting me some ice cream today," whereupon John, sitting next to her, patting the sand with his shovel, replies, "Here's a big bug."

Then there is the passive listening, with little or no overt reaction, but apparent assimilation. One finds this out with some remark a child comes up with days after the adult has made it. This moves on to listening and forming associations, but the response is the result of the child's own experience, instead of to the things he is hearing. Mature listening, of course, depends on a meeting of the minds in which one can forget oneself; here there is a genuine mental and emotional involvement with the other person. Depending upon the mood and circumstance, these different stages are apparent throughout adulthood.

Parents of the MLD child can help him move from talking to conversing, beginning always about things that are closest to the child in or out of the home. Speak in plain language, repeating the statement if you realize you have used a word that can be confusing: "This is a mean day; you will need your rubbers," will be better understood if "mean" is turned into "rainy," or "stormy." Precision is important for the MLD's comprehension; many adults get the right sense of a word through the context of the whole statement, but students as old as the PEC population often translate a statement inappropriately when some strange figure of speech or a complex phrase has been used; they do not always ask for the meaning, either, thinking they have figured it out, or preferring not to ask.

The more abstract the word is, the more difficult it is to comprehend. It is better to ask, for example, "What 'things' do you need for this lesson?" instead of what 'materials'? Or, instead of, "Your behavior is inappropriate," "Your behavior is not fitting."

MLD also have a much harder time dealing with questions that ask for a comparison of similarities, just as the non-learning disabled do. For instance, they can readily tell you how a cat and dog or a boy and man are different, but they almost always remain perplexed when asked how they are alike. After all, who pays attention to the fact that all cats and dogs have four legs, or that both the boy and the man have eyes, ears, a nose, and a mouth? To come to the simple generalization that cats and dogs are animals, or that boys and men are human beings, takes a great deal of sophistication.

Then there is the confusion that results from the different meanings that the same word has. Driving along a country road with his six-year-old MLD child, Tim, Mr. Spenser exclaimed, "There's a deer!" Tim, not having seen it, commented, "Someone you love?"

Not only is it essential to use the simplest and most explicit terms in communicating, but, whenever possible, to show by illustration; if at certain times that can't be done, spell out the details: "A deer is a large animal; it is about as big as a horse, or bigger; it has four legs," and so on.

Listen to your child, and in a way that shows him that you are completely tuned in; answer him, too, in a manner that engenders mutual respect. In these encounters, besides sharing ideas, giving directions and explanations, make sure there is plenty of room for the youngster to help make decisions. Efforts toward these ends will take lots of time and an endless amount of patience, but they are worth it.

False efforts, at inappropriate times and without spirit, as if the whole thing is a burden, will backfire. Use the natural opportunities of snack and mealtimes, walking or driving, or family social gatherings, to engage your child. His own activities (chap. 3) will provide the best fodder.

By the time the child is nine, the questions should begin to elicit more than perfunctory answers. Go beyond, "Whom did you play with today?" to, "What did you play?"; from, "Did you have a nice day?" to, "What are some of the things you did today?"; from, "Did you have a nice walk home?" to, "How did you come home?" Queries beginning with such words as "who," "what," "when" "where," "how," and "why" help to provoke thinking.

Mrs. Roman said that her conscious efforts to engage her nine-year-old Dora in a conversation were paying off. "I always think of her personal needs, naturally, but I have come to realize that almost all of our talk is about her *feelings*, with a lot of repetition, so I'm trying to create conversations that involve her more in *thinking*. I deliberately look for situations. For example, the other day I told her there was going to be a sale of coats at Belmer's tomorrow: 'It's a good time to try to get your raincoat.' "

"Goody."

"What kind do you want?"

"Like Mary's."

"What kind is that?"

"It's got a hood."

"Do you want a hood?"

"Yes."

"Why?"

"To keep my head dry."

"What color is the coat?"

"Red."

"Has it got a heavy lining?"

"Yes."

"What color?"

"Brown."

"Is it full length, below the knees, or three-quarters, like a long jacket?"

"I don't remember."

"You'd better call Mary and find out if you want one like it."

Mr. Gage said the best way he and his wife could make a worthwhile conversation with his eleven-year-old Nathan was to know a little about what he was learning in school. He and his wife went to all of the parents' meetings, and on occasion, when there was an opportunity, one of them would stop to chat with the teacher.

"We have found that keeping informed about the school activities is the easiest way to make meaningful conversation. Last night at dinner I asked, 'Still on the slaves?' "

"Yes."

"What today?"

"Underground Railroad."

"What's that?" Mrs. Gage asked.

"An underground tunnel, or like a secret road to help the slaves escape."

"Where was it?" I inquired.

"Lots of places. Rochester to Canada was one, I think."

"Who helped the slaves?" his mother asked.

"There were lots of people but today we learned about 'Harriet Toman,' or a name like that."

"Harriet Tubman?" his mother volunteered.

"Yes. She was a very brave, wonderful woman."

"Why?"

"We can go through dinner that way," Mr. Gage said, "with my wife and I helping to pull the threads together, while Nathan enjoys holding forth. When I think of those old times—Jean and I talking and he'd just sit there as if he didn't have a thought in his head. . . . Something else," Mr. Gage continued; "you know you never do anything for anyone else that doesn't turn out to be good for yourself, too. Jean and I find that we're brushing up on history and other things and learning more than we knew before. Jean's even enjoying a book about the Underground Railroad!"

Mrs. Elwood, whose daughter was eight, was excited because "Amelia really got going at dinner one night last week and it's led to all kinds of exciting things."

"How come?" Mrs. Litton asked.

"Another child brought her pet turtle to class. Then the teacher took the group to a pet store to buy one for school. *That* got to Amelia."

Mrs. Litton didn't hesitate. "Kids love pets."

"I'll say; she told us how the children and the teacher made a home for it, what it eats, about the shell, how big it is, stretching her hands out to show the size, 'that big,' and was she eager for us to get one for her. So Tom took her for it last Saturday, and has she come alive; she watches it, takes care of it, talks to it, talks to us about it —it's thrilling to see such a thing happen."

That's what comes of a good classroom activity, I thought.

WRITTEN COMMUNICATION

Words translate our thoughts; without them, ideas remain unshaped notions in our minds. The written letters out of a man's doodles, which have been assembled into various units, fix the word into a permanent state that we call "writing."

In addition to its being an essential tool, good written expression at best takes a command of language, self-confidence, a rich interior born out of sharp observations, and a feeling for adventure; if circumstances are at least partially favorable, these traits can be developed in someone confined to a wheelchair. But for many individuals, including the verbally articulate, any kind of writing is a difficult task; this is partly due to inadequate training.

There is a wide variation in the written expression of individuals, but most non-learning disabled, when left to themselves, do not write easily on their own until they are along in their teens. Still, the primary schooler is far ahead of the preschool child in storytelling, now that he can really think about the affairs of others besides his own. Also, his thoughts are more unified, for, partly, he can rely on memories that are continuous and have more order.

Still, the piecemeal quality comes out when the first and second grader tells or writes a story; usually he strings related episodes together if an instructor doesn't step in to "improve" it. For example, Helen, a seven-year-old, at home with a cold and unable to go out to play, wrote this story for her mother: "Once there was a little girl named Nancy and she went to sleep and when she woke up it was snowing and she had her breakfast and she went out to play."

Children, before the age of eleven, even when verbally articulate, usually have a great deal of difficulty expressing themselves freely in writing.

Anna, age eight, lives in a rural community near the school in which her father teaches. She is a bright and verbally articulate child.

One day Anna and I played ball together. Afterward we sat on the lawn and chatted. I invited her to tell me what she wanted to be when she grew up, and as she talked, I asked her if she minded my jotting down what she said; not only did she not mind, but she was obviously delighted.

This is the story as Anna told it to me:

"I want to be a dentist, a teacher, a ballerina, and a tap dancer. I think I'll be a dentist because I want to buy a house and furniture with the money from being a dentist or whatever. I would be a teacher to get paint for the walls—all kinds of colors and curtains. I would be a ballerina after I've been a dentist and get all the money. I would save the money being a ballerina and save it for food and stuff. I would be a tap dancer to get a china set of pretty dishes."

After Anna told her story we went into the house. She began to draw some pictures, and during that time, I asked her if she would write out the story she told me. She did not hesitate. At first she sought my help with the spelling of "mother" and "dentist" (spelling dentist wrong, nevertheless). Then I told her to never mind the spelling, so she finished without asking for further help. Notice the difference between her telling of the story and her writing of it.

Eleven-year-old Carlton's "will" was written on the occasion of a visit from Mr. Vorey, a family friend. Upon hearing a discussion about trusts and wills, Carlton joined in with, "I know the kind of will I would write."

His father smiled. "How about writing one for us?"

I am a mother now and I am
a dentest, after I am a

dentest I want to be a

Techer. and after I am a

Techer I want to be a tapda
ser and after I am a tapdaser
I want to be a baler.

My Will is the following

$400 to my mother and father

$250 to my brother

My Baseball cards to My brother,
who loves to get fingers on
them.

My Sports equipment
to my cousins

And everything else I have
the family can fight
over,

[Carl]

Carlton's piece, coming from the kind of home he did, is on the sophisticated side, although he could and often did behave very childishly. At the same time, his "will" reflects a growing detachment, and possibly a certain kind of cynicism, probably the result of a growing awareness of the imperfections of those the child looks up to —an attitude that helps the preadolescent break away from the close-bound ties to his parents.

By age thirteen or fourteen, the child who has had a good school experience and training can compose a reasonably decent report for his teacher, write imaginative stories without too much prodding, and can compose letters of a dry, factual nature, if he is so inclined. And around this time, these youngsters may secretly begin to write poems and other reflective pieces. Mamie, age thirteen, unknown to her parents, wrote a poem upon the death of her much beloved grandfather.

There are very few MLD children who do not find written expression painfully difficult; but with the kind of underpinning spelled out in much of this work, they will find it easier. One of the written rules for our PEC young adults is that all penmanship must be done in the form of printing, or what is known as manuscript. This regulation was made to fit the procedure in the PEC fieldwork placements that serve young children. There, all the writing done for the preschooler is in manuscript, following the print in the children's books; children find the unconnected letters easier to read, and, at first, to write. In most elementary schools, where manuscript is taught in the primary grades, when the child gets to be about eight or nine, he may connect his printed letters into cursive writing.

Unexpectedly, our young PEC adults who have any difficulty in coordination find it easier to print than to connect their letters. They also find printed words easier to read.

MAMIE, AGE THIRTEEN YEARS

A well respected man I start
So gentle and caring down to the heart
A quiet man some might say
But strongly missed from day to day
The great importance that he has shown
That I am so proud to have known
  And then there is his wife, so friendly and
       dear
  Such a strong lady without any fear
And as I get older and change and grow
I hope I'm like her because I envy her so
Next is his lovely daughter and son
With lots of memories of laughter and fun
What a great father they had
Giving them great years, not one bad
He's left a fine life and family I feel
And my love for him is so precious
     and real.

Feb. 21, 1962

The V̲a̲u̲l̲e̲ [value] Of Blocks

1 They help the children learning
coordination and how to learn the
difference between big and small.
Also the difference shapes and
size. And he learns that a block
is not a wapon [weapon]. Not to throw
block at orther children because
he might hurt them.

Also how to get along with orther
children. If he wants one block and
someone else has it he knows he
has to be parient [patient], and uspite [wait]
or find another block to fix it [it] insteady
of the one he wants.

May 20, 1969

What do you need to know
about
1. Blocks, How to make a good
building, that building should
have a good base. The sizes
of blocks. How to handle something
if child throws or hurt with a block.

2 Paint, To mix colors, how children
can use the bunsh, that a child
may express his feeling about
something brothering him if he
paints.

3. reading Readiness, to learn how
to write what a child wants you
to dictation. When you read a
story they learn that there
are all kinds of words. Also
numbers, how to count thingsall
around them, children, blocks, cars
ect. When going on trips reading
the signs and asking what this
says. That the book is, interest, age
of children, length, attrictive, and good picture

Don't fuss over the mechanics of writing—that is, the shapes of the letters, punctuation, or spelling, until the child has finished expressing his thoughts in the composition; and even at that, depending upon how much of a chore it is, go easy on the corrections; confine them only to what is most important—probably places where there should be capital letters and periods. The essential job is to get the child to want to record his ideas with some satisfaction.

At best, as with the young non-learning disabled, it is hard for the MLD to think of anything to write about. As in verbal expression, ideas emerge from activities and interests, a number of which have been presented above: listening to stories, reading, clubs, socials, holidays and other festivities, visits, trips, and so on. Keeping a bulletin board where the child can tack up postcards, letters received, cutouts, and his own writings, and expressing your interest in them, will stimulate his interest. After all, the main point in writing is to convey a message; if the child knows he can do that he will be motivated to write.

First steps in writing can start with the child's writing his own name and address on large labels or things he possesses. (It is significant that when our young adults first enter the PEC Program, many do not think of writing their names on anything they own, including their homework.) Then the child can help you with your shopping list, or write one of his own when he accompanies you, write brief telephone messages as well as jotting down messages for you when he goes out; he can also be encouraged to write brief thank-you notes and short letters to family and friends and brief greetings at holiday time. Fun will be added if he is encouraged to decorate the greeting notes.

Story dictation, on a more elaborate level than previously, is also helpful to the MLD in the primary and grade school. From first grade up, the process can be a cooperative effort, begun by any child who is ready to speak up, or by the teacher, if necessary, and then finished off by other children. It's profitable, besides, to have the pupils copy the finished tale into their notebooks—another aid to reading, writing, and spelling. As the child matures, and his interests broaden, his stories expand as well as become more formalized.

ARITHMETIC

Quantitative experiences are prevalent in man's life. No matter who he is or where he lives, they are the basis for mathematical figurings: when, how many, how few, how big, how little, how near, how far—these, among others, are key questions to arithmetical thinking.

If the suggestions mentioned earlier are followed, the MLD will have a better foundation for operating formal numbers in the later grades. Indeed, these quantitative concepts are pursued with the non-learning disabled throughout their elementary-school lives, but with the methodology changing in accordance with the child's development.

Whether at home or school, MLD children will need to relate their calculations to tangible objects. Some learning devices in the various areas are:

Quantity: counting discs, abacus, fact-finders, number frames, number charts, flannel board, number-cutouts, domino cards, dominoes, dial telephone, fractional parts, money.
Time: calendar, clock, metronome, watch.
Sizes: ruler, yardstick [especially made for the beginner], tape

measure, speedometer, square-inch cards, foot cards, yard cards.

Weight: balances, spring scales, grocers' scales, nurses' scales, boxes, containers, sand, fruit, beans.

Volume: eight-ounce, pint, quart, and gallon measures; pans, bottles, spoons, and cups; quart, peck, and bushel measures; baskets and boxes. *

Use any regular objects that tie symbols to things, and through which they can be compared, added to, or taken away from—the basic processes that also involve multiplication and division.

Don't waste your time worrying about the arithmetic you think your child should know, but do pay attention to the basic concepts that he will need in managing his life, and do plot ways to help him learn them. Wherever he goes, take advantage of the never-ending display of figures that confront all of us on houses, telephones, license numbers, streets, letters, and price tags, among other things.

If parents could see the inability and embarrassment of many of our PEC young adults in making purchases that involve the simplest forms of money, they would take every opportunity to induct the MLD child, as early in his life as possible, into the use of coins and bills, keeping in mind, though, that the average child is about six before he begins to have any real sense of its value. In a study of allowances that I did, I was amazed at the vagueness and confusion of bright eight-year-olds in the handling of their twenty-five- to fifty-cent weekly allowances. Preschoolers, who play store and exchange money, are simply going through the motions, so far as any comprehension of its real value is concerned.

Daily activities can present good opportunities for meaningful problem solving, if the adult keeps his eyes

* Christine P. Ingram, *Education of the Slow-Learning Child* (New York: Ronald Press, 1960), pp. 329 and 330.

and ears open. At the airport, a seven-year-old re-marked, "The plane looks like a little bird."

"Yes; watch what happens when it gets closer."

"It's getting bigger."

"Yes. Let's count how many people get off."

Eight-year-old Jane cried, "Look at the big bunch of birds on the wire."

"Yes. Let's count them."

"Let's see how many fly away."

The comments can run on: "Just a few flew away"; or, "A lot"; another time "bunch" could be introduced again, with, "Let's see how many flowers are in this bunch."

Grace, age ten: "I need stamps for my invitations."

"How many?"

"Six."

"We'll have to buy them at the post office. You pay for them."

"How much?"

"Each stamp costs ten cents. You figure it out. If you have trouble, I'll help you."

Steve, thirteen, told his mother that the new blotter they had bought for his desk was too big to fit into the frame.

"Get the yardstick on my sewing machine, and the shears are on top, too. Measure the blotter, and cut it to fit. Call me if you need help."

Using a ruler is an indispensable need at some mo-ments in everyone's life. Begin with an extra-large mea-suring rod that is especially designed for your MLD child; mark off only the inch and the half-inch, at first, with well-defined numbers and lines. Most of our MLD young adults have great trouble using the ruler with any precision, simply because they have never been properly taught. It is not an easy process for some of them, but they all finally learn it; and if they had been taught earlier and gradually, they would find it much easier.

Clock time is an utter necessity; some of our PEC students have trouble with the seconds and minutes between the hour. They not only need to learn to read the clock as children, but also to build up a sense of time; this comes more easily with the kind of routine and schedule discussed earlier.

Many parents of the MLD want to know at about what age children should learn the processes of addition, subtraction, multiplication, and division. While such a chart can be helpful as a guide, it is important to realize that many schools are moving away from a grade placement of these topics, with the child being taught them as his experiences or activities require. Playing store in the third grade, for example, could entail some kind of multiplication before the formal process has been introduced in class. The danger in depending on activity alone is that even the bright child can move up in the grades with great gaps in his arithmetical knowledge; and the MLD child, who is slower to begin with, is more handicapped than ever unless the process involves an orderly progression of steps.

For the MLD purposes then, the grade and age levels in learning the main processes in arithmetic that have been commonly adopted in the schools in the past are presented below.*

In the first grade, age six: addition and subtraction of one-place numbers, up to ten, with an understanding of

---

* Bureau of Elementary Curriculum Development, *The Elementary School Curriculum: An Overview* (New York State Education Department, 1954).

the meaning behind the digit, separately and in groups; they also *begin* to work with and comprehend the meanings of penny, nickel, dime, and such coins as are useful in their daily lives; they begin to gain concepts of size and comparison.

Second graders, age seven: addition of single columns to about eighteen; two-column addition and subtraction, without carrying and borrowing; exposure to simple reasoning problems; they also learn to tell time, and to work with simple measurements that are required in making things for holiday and other activities.

Third graders, age eight: move on to addition and subtraction of three-place numbers; zero and borrowing are included; work with money within the limits of about one dollar; addition and subtraction are related to simple multiplication and division; the simple fractions of one-half, one-fourth, one-third, and one-fifth are introduced.

Fourth graders, age nine: learn to make change up to about five dollars; identify a square, rectangle, triangle, circle; there is an extension of all multiplication and division combinations; multiplication is extended to three-place numerals by three; one-place division is presented in the formal written form with uneven answers.

Fifth graders, age ten: work with all reasonable types of multiplication; division includes up to three-digit division; work with length, liquid, and dry measure; add and subtract common fraction, using the common denominator.

Sixth graders, age eleven: refine and continue to extend the above processes, and also that of problem solving.

The above sequence has been laid out in a cut-and-dried pattern for easy assimilation, but within it the four processes—addition, subtraction, multiplication, and division—are interlocking. Working with concrete materials, such as rods or pencils, the able MLD can take in the fact that 3 plus 2 equals 5, just as 5 take away 3 equals 2; or that 2 times 2 equals 4, just as 4 can be divided by 2 twice. But the MLD who has trouble with this linked approach should be taught one process at a time.

It is also good teaching to make profitable use of an experience that the child is having before the grade in which it is designated. If, for instance, before the fourth grade (see above) the child is building with blocks that involve squares, rectangles, and other shapes, casually make it a conscious learning experience. Label the shelves with the names of the shapes beside the drawings of them; and as the child takes the blocks off the shelves, offer an appropriate comment, such as, "You are building with squares and rectangles"; or, "Those two square blocks are the length of that one rectangular block."

Concrete materials should be bountifully used through all of the grades; also, problem-solving needs to be an integral part of the curriculum. It is well to note, too, that although the metric system is not yet part of our lives, it is gradually being introduced in the primary grades of most schools.

Various publishing houses and manufacturers of rehabilitation materials and equipment are now putting out all kinds of aids to help promote learning skills in various subjects, including that of arithmetic. Those I have seen are well thought out and can be very useful, but *only* as they relate to, and can be actively involved with, the problem solving in the youngster's everyday life. There is little advantage to have him play with make-believe money, for example, unless he really buys and pays for some things himself. Without real-life experiences, these materials become games that are sterile and mechanical.

DEVELOPING INNER RESOURCES

Most adults, as they mature, realize how woefully lost the individual is who lacks inner resources. This may take the form of always having to be on the go, constantly surrounding oneself with people, or being glued to TV. For the MLD, it usually means being alone, with television as the sole companion.

For all of us, learning handicapped or not, the time to begin developing inner resources is early rather than late. Whatever their sex, the PEC young adults who lead the most satisfactory lives are those who have developed some skill in at least one activity: cooking, crocheting, knitting, sewing, gardening, playing at sports, or collecting items; these and other things are a source of satisfaction only if the MLD individual does not feel that perfection is required.

A pet for which the child can be completely responsible possibly by the time he is fourteen, and who is dependent on him for care and love, can be a great source of joy, too. Also, there are many clubs, now, for the learning disabled, with such appropriate functions as trips, dances, movies, sports, and, best of all, the chance to make friends and team up with the opposite sex. If an appropriate club is not available in your vicinity, get in touch with your religious leader, the school principal, or the Association for Children with Learning Disabilities to connect with other parents who have similar needs.

The best way for the child to find himself is through his interest in the accomplishments he enjoys, and friends. These are achievements that grow over the years; they take effort and hard work on the part of both the parents and the child, but they pay off, saving the MLD individual from the common lifetime affliction of loneliness.

5

Sparking
and Maintaining
Teenage Interests

Childhood, adolescence, maturity: each stage brings a different self to the same subject, grasping it in such different ways that the matter becomes transformed from level to level.

Reading *Alice's Adventures in Wonderland* at age twenty opens more doors to it than at age twelve; *War and Peace* takes on a different significance when one has piled on some years. So it is with any subject; a study of plant life at age eight, as a high-school freshman, and later in college presents such different vistas that one can forget that one has studied it before. Thus an endless list of themes, in the hands of the imaginative, innovative teacher, turns into an exciting adventure for the pupil, at whatever age level.

At any time, it is futile to attempt explanations that are based on a logic distant from the student's mental stage. Showing a four-year-old how electricity works in making a bell ring, however well he memorizes and verbalizes, does not shut off his own unconscious belief in a magical explanation. Children, like adults, also believe what they see. A thirteen-year-old, after a study of Europe, wrote that the distance from Holland to the foot of Italy's boot was "a couple of hours journey by car." Good teaching can overcome such misconceptions.

Like all children, the MLD find knowledge an exciting adventure when the teacher is caring, inventive, and resourceful. Years later, I can still hear the thrill in the voice of a disadvantaged MLD student, age eighteen, when she exclaimed to her PEC environmental science teacher, "You mean that a chicken is a *bird!*" The cooperating school that helped PEC train her as a teacher aide reported that Lita, who could barely read when she came into the PEC Program, "ate up many of the books in the elementary-school library." This young lady is now working in a paid job as a teacher aide and doing very satisfactorily.

The inventive teacher will turn any subject into a fountainhead for the three Rs, but, again, the experiential approach, as the MLD grow older, is essential. The experience must expand not only with increasing age and capacity, but it must also take into account the individual's background. The study of a geographical location and its resources, for example, should be different for the child raised in an agrarian culture from that of a city dweller.

However, considerations are often ignored by the teacher who rigidly latches her instruction to a textbook, or the child's memorization of facts. Under any circumstances, a good memory is a blessing, but without understanding, it remains a parrot's exercise. Besides, the books from which the MLD study are too frequently inappropriate, being either meant for the non-learning disabled, or simply revised into watered-down texts, with the facts diminished into nothingness. Whatever the system, good instructors can accomplish miracles; I have yet to see a superior teacher who is not superior with any class, or the inept who wasn't inept with whatever grade he instructed.

A good example of shortchanging students comes to my mind as I recall my observation of a class of fourteen-year-old "slow learners" a few years ago in a public school; I was told it was a model of excellence, and went there with high expectations. As I entered the room, the teacher was telling the visibly well behaved and orderly class that "this morning we are going to learn about the ear." At the front of the room was a large, professionally drawn chart that portrayed this valuable sensory organ, with its various parts labeled: outer ear, auditory canal, anvil, stirrup, around to the cochlea, and so on.

Touching each label with her pointer, the teacher clearly pronounced them aloud, having the class repeat in unison. Then she explained the function of each part, calling on various pupils to echo an explanation that was obviously not comprehended. Next she warned the class about the danger to the ear of infection, loud noise, and she emphasized the necessity of keeping the ears clean. The learning disabled, who have reason to worry more about their body intactness than other adolescents, could only have found such a dour approach demoralizing.

At the end of this dull and meaningless lesson, the teacher handed out a sheet of neat, carefully mimeographed homework. On the left side of the paper was a column listing the names of the various parts of the ear; vertically opposite, but out of order, was a line describing their individual functions. The assignment called for each student to draw a line from the name of each part of the ear across to the explanation that fit. Not one student asked a single question during the entire lesson.

A study of the different sensory organs, including the

ear, *is* useful, particularly for the MLD; the focus, however, should be on how much better and richer life is when the organ is fully used. Where the ear is concerned, hearing is not necessarily listening, any more than seeing is necessarily looking; I have found it great fun to work from those theories, in both the primary and junior high schools.

I can't think of any subject that should be studied in isolation; certainly the ear connects with all of the other sensory organs. The children should have been asked what they were, and a pupil should have written them on the board, with the others helping with the spelling when necessary.

Essential to the comprehension of *any* student in the subject of the ear is the understanding that all sounds are motions or vibrations, that they are all different, and that sound gets from one place to another—is conducted —through the air. One easy and enjoyable way to show the vibration is having students tap a toy drum at the edge while feeling it vibrate with the free hand; or they might put some grains of cereal on the parchment and watch what happens as they tap the edge.

The blindfold technique is profitable, too. One student could create a sound by tapping a glass with a spoon, shaking a rattle, plucking a guitar string, or whatever he chooses. If the blindfolded student's ears do not identify the sound, he can touch or smell the instrument to see what other senses help. Which sense is most helpful to the ear? Are the same ones equally helpful for every sound? The MLD will invent their own procedures and with great enthusiasm as they find the answers.

Finally, the drawing of the ear could be presented, but the diagram should show only the parts that are necessary to the understanding of its function, with simple labels: probably the outer ear, the passageway to the eardrum, the three little bones in the middle ear, and the inner ear. The explanation should make clear how the vibrations are sent to the brain.

Homework can often consist of any number of engaging exercises. One might be to have the students listen to the various sounds they can hear during a half hour in the morning, in the afternoon, and at night. One or more of these questions might be answered, depending on the level of the class: Which half hour had the most noises? Why? Or, the student could write a paragraph about which sound was the most interesting and why. These questions will take thinking that includes listening, noticing, counting and figuring, reading, writing, spelling, and undoubtedly, verbal communication; meanwhile, the students enjoy what they are learning.

At home, the subject can have different possibilities, with the parents entering into the spirit of inquiry. Once the excitement has worn off, the exploration of another sensory organ should be undertaken until each is covered; it's fun, too, to tackle them in combination.

Another time, some teenagers' interests needed to be sparked and maintained in a high school for "slow learners," where the sophomore class was bored and unruly, but, finally, we hit upon an activity that awoke their enthusiasm; they were to create a supply store for the school. In this, we felt that the students could be useful and active, while, at the same time, the project could supply the means for extending their knowledge in various academic subjects.

After the sophomores met with the other school classes several times, they drew up a list of the suggested supplies: varieties of pencils, pens, paper, pads, notebooks, covers, erasers, rulers, and so on. The other classes also requested T-shirts, briefcases, balls, checkers, and other materials and equipment for games and sport; and finally, sweets.

Soon the sophomores found that they had to divide themselves up into various committees; they labeled them Purchasers, Bookkeepers, Shopkeepers, Salesmen, and Distributors; then they chose the one they wanted to be on. With fifteen students in the class, there were not more than two or three on a committee—a manageable number. Each group chose its own chairman, who met, when necessary, with the class teachers; the entire class met weekly.

From the time of the idea's inception, working several hours a day, it took four weeks to open the shop, but it was at least two months before all of the supplies were in. The stock was constantly enlarged upon, with various class requests, such as things for gifts at holiday times.

The success of the venture would have been impossible without the full support of the school and the sophomore teacher, Mrs. Berns, and her assistant, Mr. Feldor. To begin with, the school supplied all of the needed money, but the appropriate committees bought all of the supplies, distributed them, kept charge of the expenditures and income, with, of course, great support and supervision from Berns and Feldor. Both teachers said they found the going very rough at times, and occasionally despaired, but by the end of the year, they reported that they believed the project should be a permanent part of the sophomore curriculum. As anticipated, the project resulted in increased amounts of verbal and written communication, with arithmetic also getting its full share. The social studies area fared much better than we thought possible, centering around the sophomores' purchase of paper, leather, ink, carbon paper, and so forth: "Where did the products come from? Where were they made and how?" were the leading questions. (Not one student, incidentally, nor did the teachers, know what the composition of ink was.)

The parents of the children in the other classes caught

the sophomore spirit from their own offspring far better than hearing the teachers' reports at the monthly meeting. One result was that a couple, whose daughter was good at handiwork, organized, with several other enthusiastic parents, a "Hand-Made Things Club"—the title their children gave it. The HMTC, as it came to be called, involved the students not only in handiwork itself, but also in the selection of materials, in purchasing them, in all kinds of verbal communication, and in the handling of money. This venture ended up being part of the home economics curriculum.

Another couple, the somewhat discouraged parents of Burk James, a junior, who was generally very contentious, was inspired enough by these activities to find a wholly new idea. Mr. James, a businessman himself, persuaded three stores in the business district of the small city in which the family lived to allow his son to distribute the weekly sales-leaflets in the neighborhood. The stores combined to pay Burk a small weekly fee, with Mr. James, unknown to his son, adding two dollars of his own, the allowance the boy formerly got. The father asked the stores to hold the son accountable for the number of leaflets distributed, to how many homes, and the number of hours he spent on the job.

The venture started for Burk when the manager of the store where the family shopped called Burk and asked him if he would undertake the job of distributing the leaflets. When Burk brought the news to his parents, his attitude, at first, was a kind of groan: "Wellll, if they need me." He surely showed no enthusiasm; secretly, the Jameses thought, among other things, that the idea scared their son. But with Mr. James, Burk went to meet each of the three store managers, at which time the routes were mapped out and the business discussed.

After that, Mr. James kept in the background, until one day, several months after Burk had been distributing the flyers, he brought one to his parents, exclaiming, "Don't you think this thing would be better if it read, 'SPECIAL! A KNOCKDOWN ON COATS,' instead of 'COAT SALE!' " The Jameses, needless to say, were thrilled.

From then on, Burk continued making all kinds of suggestions about how to improve the ads; over the year and a half that he worked at the job, his suggestions were adopted three times.

"I know it sounds like a fairy story," his mother told several parents at graduation, "but there was the printer of the flyers telling Mr. Cone, the manager of the Town Food Market, to send Burk in about a job after graduation. The job will start with lots of legwork, but who cares? Burk said he'd take it if he had to stand on his head! It really is a fairy story," she repeated.

"But you and your husband worked very hard behind the scenes, didn't you?" I asked. "Doesn't such a fairy story need parents' help?"

"I'll say." Then, laughingly, Mrs. James said, tapping the top of her head, "But don't forget that Burk had it up here. *He* made it work."

"He got the right chance," another parent sensibly concluded.

6

A Program
for Young MLD Adults
and
Its Implications

CREATING OUT OF
DISCOURAGEMENT

It was a cool June day in 1965, blowy but fresh. I walked
up Second Avenue in New York with the echo of my
previous day's graduation message still ringing in my
ears. It ended, "The stars will shine brightly for you."

Poetic, maybe, I thought, but do I really believe that?
Wasn't I trying to make the students and their parents
feel good? There they sat, the few "slow-learner" graduates, listening attentively, well-scrubbed, in their ties and
jackets, and foamy white dresses, looking like magazine
ads for cereal and soap. But I know that their parents
were watching from their uncomfortable chairs with
a complicated mixture of feelings about their "exceptional" children graduating from an "exceptional"

164

school. It had been painful going all the way up through the years; barefoot on the sharp stones would have been easier than the bruises on their spirits. "Now what?" some of them asked me.

"Now what?" The question awoke the nightmare of my own childhood, much of which had been spilled over into my school life. Limping from subject to subject until the fifth grade, I finally stayed back, and was then put into a group with the children who could not manage in the regular class. In secondary school I continued to be a terrified and lonely failure, although my feelings no longer broke out into periods of rash and aggressive behavior.

I graduated at the bottom of my high-school class of 250. But not long before graduation, I was touched by my first angel. And while it would take a long time before I could begin to use anything near my full potential, I had placed my foot on the first rung of the ladder. The new step for me was connected with Lois Turner, a teacher I had in my senior year. One day, after I had been in her class for about a month, she asked me to stay after the others left, saying, "I want to speak with you." My inner self curled into a tight knot.

"Now, what do you see as you sit and look out of that window every week?" Miss Turner smiled as she comfortably settled into the chair next to me. With that "Now, what?" question, with its obvious interest in *me*, the years of withheld tears fell over my face.

So, the "Now, what?" asked by afflicted parents touched on my old wounds. No wonder I'm here, I thought, weaving my way up the sidewalk of the broad avenue that had come alive with the early morning traffic. I meant what I said in that graduation talk. I've got to help the stars shine for their children. But beneath my well-practiced coat of assurance my timidity was having another field day. Breathing in deeply, and letting go

165

slowly, a way that I had recently learned to relax, I walked into the supermarket; I wasn't wrong in guessing that the early nine-o'clock opening would quickly see me to the man in charge.

"Would you need any help from a high-school graduate?" I asked.

"Boy?"

"Boy or girl."

"Live around here?"

"Maybe or maybe not, but they're in a nearby school; they know the neighborhood."

"What school?"

"The _____ School."

"Huh. *That* place! They're real dumb kids."

"No, they're not."

"That's what people say; they're wild. What's wrong with them? You the principal?"

I disregarded the last question, and was unprepared for the first. "They learn more slowly, but they're *not* dumb."

"Look, lady, I've got enough trouble with the *un*-slow learners working here. Be nice and go away," he said, turning to open a crate of lettuce.

My attempts at the neighborhood florist and antique shops were no more successful; if anything, the florist was less kind in his remarks.

When the chairman of the board of the "high school" in question had called me three years before to plead that I volunteer my services as educational consultant to his school for "slow learners," I never expected that I would be making these efforts that day. Not that he, or anyone else, for that matter, had assigned this postgraduate concern to me. The entreaty that I come, I was told, was because of my reputation as a teacher and a tutor of children before I became a professor at the university.

"We need a child development expert," the board chairman said, "someone who knows the whole child first, and who doesn't treat his learning problem as if that's all that there is to him; someone whose mind isn't so full of retardation that it makes every child retarded who's got a learning disability." The chairman was obviously bitter.

But I declined the invitation several times. First of all, my university teaching and various other responsibilities took nearly all of my time; second, although I knew that my background was extraordinarily broad, I felt that there must be a body of knowledge about the "slow learner" of which I knew next to nothing.

Nevertheless, the chairman's persistence finally got me to visit and observe the classes, and the next thing I knew, I was listening to the staff discuss its problems. Surprisingly, I found myself completely at home in the entire situation, finding that many of the difficulties of the teachers of this population, although on a larger scale, were not dissimilar to those I had experienced in my teaching and tutoring experiences in the regular private and public schools.

Additionally, visits in and around the city, to the other few exceptional schools, convinced me that the situation was critical. So, I set to work in the _____ School. But I wasn't there very long when another crucial question broke in: "Where do the students go when they get out of here?"

Ironically, the question was more relevant to the most academically able in the class; these students were not suitable for the government workshops, where the training is in mechanical and manipulative skills and is meant for the less academically able. Government support, since the early sixties, was increasingly providing much needed opportunities for the retarded, but the "slow learner" was completely overlooked. Neither did jobs like packaging use their best abilities. At the same time they had not the ability to qualify for a regular university program. "The result," as a parent put it to me "is that they sit all day and look at TV and wither away. If they're not doing that, they are mad and frustrated and we parents are just as mad with frustration."

This heartless experience of trying to get them jobs is just a perpetuation of life's nibble at the spirit of these "slow learners," I thought. What will adulthood do to them?

I wanted to help. Parents had approached me many times, and I had already turned an exciting idea over in my head—but I was afraid it could not be carried out. Nevertheless, out of desperation, as much as anything else, and with the chairman of the board's persistent urging, I made my plans.

By this time I knew no graduate program existed anyplace that trained "slow learners" for a professional life in a consistent and structured way and was more than a hit-or-miss affair. In fact, I had knocked at some doors in special education already, trying unsuccessfully to get others interested; in truth, were I not so tenacious, I'd have given up the idea.

At last I made up my mind to move ahead; I would try an experiment with two of the _____ School graduates, educating and training them to be teacher aides in the helping professions; and while I knew there would be much prejudice and many obstacles to overcome, I would begin the training in nursery schools.

The idea of utilizing preschool settings for moving these young adults into the helping professions was not happenstance, nor simply because of my previous connections. Rather, it took into account my experience in the preschools, and up and down all of the grades, from which I found the early childhood teachers, generally, the most knowledgeable about the child's development

—not surprising, perhaps, in that the greatest fund of knowledge in human growth pertains to the early years. Moreover, they also appeared to be most sympathetic and caring in their attitudes toward children.

Then, as much as, or more than anything else, I knew the good nursery school could provide these particular young adults with some of the essential concepts that their own earlier school experiences had neglected. The work of our PEC students, as will soon be seen, constantly bears out this hypothesis. For example, through exposure to block building they learn about size, shape, reference, and comparison; and as they become more alert to the ways of children and other forms of life, they increase their powers of observation, as well as learning new patterns of responsibility.

In the long run, my old previous school connections, the one thing I felt sure I could count on and which ultimately proved to be essential to the success of the experiment, did stand me in good stead; even at that, however, there were moments of secret tears, and times when my heart failed me.

The first two schools that I approached, like most of those I had taught in, had educators of the highest order; still, while they did not turn me away, there was an initial reluctance that I had more than anticipated. Nor could it have been otherwise; their first responsibility was to the children and their parents, and those involvements were already very great. In addition, they knew nothing about the "exceptional," or "slow learner"; and like most of the population-at-large, the teachers and directors drew from the stereotype of the extremely retarded that had been flagrantly held up to the public view for so many years.

Most unfortunate of all, I, myself, had not been able to dig up any reliable information about the cause of these "slow learners' " difficulties that would enlighten

Cognitive Development
Through Block Building Activity

9A Shapes of blocks
    A. Name the shapes

good

1. Root Board
2. Ramp
3. Gohic Door
4. Large triangle
5. Small triangle
6. Quarter Circle

7. half Circle
8. Large Switch
9. Large Column
10 small column
11. Small Curve
12. Small Arch
13. Large Arch

9B. Give three ways children learn the shape

good

1. by seeing
2. Building
3. feeling & touching
4. Putting them away

[Do they hear them?
  When?]

10A. Sizes of blocks
    . Name the sizes

Yes

1. Small   Whole
2. Medium   half
3. Large   Quarter

10B Give three ways children learn the sizes

good

1. Side by side
2. on top when building
3. seeing

[Do they compare
  them? When? How?]

THIS DEMONSTRATES A STUDENT'S BECOMING ALERT TO OTHER FORMS OF LIFE—AND RESPONSIBILITY.

Animals and Plants In
the Classroom

1.What animals and plants do you have
in your classroom?

1. We have a guinea pig and a spider plant.

2. Children learn how to observe animals
and plants through seeing, hearing smelling
and touching. Give one example for each sense.

2. Animals-and Plants.
Through seeing they can see the animals +
plants grow

2 Animals and Plants
Through hearing they could only hear the
animals more around, eating and squeaking.

6. Animals and Plants.
Through smelling they could smell the odor
of the animal and can smell certain plants.

2. Animals and Plants
Through touching they could feel the
different furs and wleth of the animals.
And feel the different texture of plants.

3. Children learn how to help the growth of animals and plants. How? Give more then one way.

3. Care for <u>animals</u> is to feed it right, a clean home and affection.

3 Care for <u>plants</u> is to give it the right light it needs, to give it water when dry. The right soil and maybe plant food.

4. They learn life can reproduce itself. How? Give more then one way.

4. With <u>Animals</u> they can learn that they have babies
And that <u>plants</u> grow babies flowers.
shoots

5. They learn about death? How? Give more then one way.

5. When a classroom pet dies, its good to talk about it.
When a plant die of bad care again its good to talk about it.
Again if a child has a pet at home it good to <u>decuess</u> it, or <u>seening</u> one in a park.
Seeing a plant <u>ripe</u> out of the <u>grown</u> you can talk about it.

6. They learn to be responsible. How? Give more then one way.

6. Animals - By having a job to take care of the animals, by ~~give~~ it food. And to take it home on weekend. ✓

6. Plants- By giving it water and light, to be their job. And to watch out for the plants. ✓

7. They learn to care about life. How? Give more then one way.

7. They learn by feeding and giving the <u>animals</u> a good home and a ~~ffection~~. ✓

7. They lean to take care of <u>plants</u> by watering and giving the right light. ✓

8. Can anyone know all about life and death? Explain your answer.

8. No, Because there is <u>to</u> much to know.

them, any more than it did me. I could only offer them my own hunches and assurances about Wilma and Clara, whom I was asking them to train; the young women were fond of children, well put together, and despite their learning difficulties, had many untapped strengths. Still, had I not had the trust and respect of these professionals—and I failed with some others, even so—there is no doubt that I would have had an even harder time in getting a foothold in the schools.

As it was, each one agreed to try the experiment with me for the fall term, suggesting that in January I should transfer them to two other schools—a suggestion I immediately acted upon, finding two other nursery settings that were willing to take over after the initial thrust. But when January came, the two schools that cooperated in the original experiment asked to keep Wilma and Clara for the remainder of the year. The two students had proved to be very helpful; also, as the teachers became fond of them, they grew increasingly interested in their learning problems.

In my home that year, in a block of free time that I set aside from my university responsibilities, I tutored both students; also, I went about building a curriculum for their educational and professional needs, having little faith, though, as I saw the prejudice among most of my own professional colleagues, that anything substantial could grow out of my efforts; yet I felt sure I could help the two students, win over the schools in which they were being trained, and publish some articles for public consumption, thus alerting other professionals. Always at the back of my head was Lois Turner, the teacher who saved my life.

Word travels quickly on the grapevine; other parents of "slow learners," and their children, were clamoring for the same opportunity that Wilma and Clara were getting; I couldn't have stopped had I wanted to. By the fall, I had seven students under my wing—too large a group for my home; in any case, feeling that the experiment now needed a more professional climate, I began to use my university office during my off-hours.

There I was most interested in the fact that when my colleagues did not know who the students were (with the exception of one who was extremely neurologically impaired, whom we were trying out for a special reason), they assumed they belonged to the university community. When I found an opportunity to discuss the teacher aide experiment, their ignorance of the MLD made it impossible for them to accept the idea; neither would they come to observe, to find out what was going on—a sad commentary on educators who profess to have an open mind.

Still, there were always heartening exceptions, among them the then chairman of my department. When I made note of my extracurricular activities in the yearly report, he took an immediate interest; and the next year, with the dean's approval, I was released from two of my child development courses to pursue the experiment.

Some ten years later, New York University, with the help of devoted parents and friends, established the Para-Educator Center for Young Adults. By that time, the curriculum was firmly established, with a devoted and conscientious staff to implement it; and from the two original cooperating schools, there are now twenty-nine, some of which have *asked* to train the PEC students. A number of the schools that can afford to hire the aides after training is completed are doing so. Other day-care centers, nursery and public schools are also hiring them.

CATCHING UP ON LOST CONCEPTS

The choice of using the nursery school for training the PEC students in the helping professions has produced gratifying results. One that delights our hearts has been in the changing attitudes of the cooperating schools themselves. Threatened, at first, by a population of which they were totally ignorant, and knowing only the caricature of the retarded, they were anxious about exposing their preschoolers to the situation; also they were worried about the reactions of the preschoolers' parents. Interestingly enough, when parents came to realize that the PEC aide was from a special program, it turned out that a few of them had an MLD child of their own. Besides, the teachers quickly saw that most MLD had great possibilities; there were exceptions, of course, but the proportion was no greater than those among the regular university population whom I had trained to be regular teachers.

As already indicated, when I began the program, I reasoned that, in the nursery school settings, the MLD would catch up on some of the concepts they had missed in their early school years. The child study classes constantly show how this process works. In the one I teach, PEC students report on their fieldwork, partly by reading from daily logs that they keep.

In one, Jayne reported, "I watched my group of four-year-olds make Jell-O with Miss Abst. She calls everything to the children's attention. They talked about the color, 'like cherries.' Herb said, 'It looks like colored sand.' When the hot water went on it, Jill said, 'It's melting like snow.'

Today Miss ___ started to do the planting of our garden. Each child got a chance to put some soil in to the basket. We used soil from the bag then we took the children outside to dig for soil because we didn't have enough soil for our garden. Then Miss ___ took out different kinds of seeds. The children looked at the different seeds with a magnifying glass. The children noticed that some seeds are big and some were small. They also noticed that some seeds were long and some were round. Then each children got a chance to water our garden. Then we put the garden by the window so the seeds would grow. We are going to look at our garden every day to see if see if anything has happened yet. We will water our garden every other day.

"All the children in the group tasted it before Miss Abst put it in the refrigerator. The next day when we had it for lunch, Miss Abst said, 'Look what happened to the Jell-O when it was in the refrigerator.' One of the children thought it was 'just like jelly.' " Then Jayne added thoughtfully, "Who would ever have thought there was anything to learn from Jell-O?"

"Yeah, and at four years of age," Pam added. "All I ever did was eat it."

Miller followed with: "My fives went on the Staten Island Ferry last week. The teacher, Miss Rodney, showed them lots of pictures of what they would see, and she explained all about the ferry boat. Then, the day after we got back, the class had a discussion about what they saw. Now, in block building, some of the children don't do anything but the Harbor. They put in Governor's Island, Staten Island, the Statue of Liberty, the tip of Manhattan, tugs—you can't believe it."

"Maybe we can take that trip in environmental science, someday," Rhea suggested.

Another time, Rhea told our child study class about a very interesting experience her five-year-old class had: "Mrs. Merchant took them out into the yard to see some old pipes that had been torn out of the basement. She asked the children what they thought they were for. Their answers were funny.

"One boy said, 'Mice could go down in them.'

"Another said, 'Water.'

"Katrina said, 'We could blow in them.'

"I guess Mrs. Merchant didn't think the answers were so funny," Rhea continued, "because she said the children had given some good answers—that things *did* go down pipes; and you can blow in them the way you do in musical instruments."

"Now imagine a five-year-old being that smart," Morey said.

Rhea made no comment, but went on: "Then the teacher took the class down into the basement. Mr. Kelley, the superintendent, showed them the new pipes, and how they connected to the boiler, and told them how the water boiled and sent the steam heat into the building."

"I was always afraid to go into our basement when I was a child," Jenny, another student, put in. The class laughed, as if understanding.

"Wait. I'm not finished yet," Rhea objected. "The very next day, Mrs. Merchant boiled up some water in the steam kettle on the electric burner. The children saw the steam come out of the spout. Then, turning to the class, she asked, 'How many of you ever thought of steam in pipes making heat?' "

"Do you think the children understood all of that?" Melvin asked.

"I'll bet they got some of it," Claire retorted.

"It's a very good beginning," I answered, asking, at the same time, "Was it better for the children to learn that way, or to be told about it?"

The class had no doubt of the answer.

One report added a very important element to our discussions: Marva began by telling how, in her fours, Sylvia came to school and told how "Daddy let me put some grass seeds in the ground."

"The next day, Mrs. Irwin came with a chart she got out of a seed catalog. It showed the seed growing under the earth, and she explained all about it.

"That afternoon, while some of the children were in music, we took the others to the florist shop around the corner. We got earth and seed and flowerpots. It's cute the way the children think it's an honor to carry something," she laughed.

"The day after that," she continued, "the two of us and the assistant helped the children plant the seeds.

Each of them were given a pot with the earth we had already put in it. And would you believe that a child asked, 'If I swallow a seed will grass grow in me?' " Various students expressed amazement.

"Why does that surprise you?" I asked.

"How could any child think such a silly thing?" Jenny was scornful.

"Wait," I cautioned. "Isn't there a kind of magic about grass or anything else growing out of a seed? Even at your age, when you read about something magic, or see some silly stuff on TV, don't you sometimes think it could happen to you?"

"Like Alice in Wonderland," Nita smiled. "I used to be afraid I would shoot up like that."

"Listening to children's comments," I added, "teaches us how they think; they do not think the same way adults do."

The class was quiet and thoughtful.

In the spring, during a thaw, Harry reported how, during a play period, his group of fours and fives waded into two small pools of water, where the cement was buckling in the yard. One pool was in the shade of the shed that housed the outdoor equipment, the other in the middle of the yard, where the sun hit it for most of the day. Miss Denton asked the children to look at the two pools. "They could see right away that one was bigger than the other, and when she said, 'Let's watch and see which pool dries up first,' they seemed interested. But then the weather changed and we couldn't go out for a few days.

"But she didn't let them forget about it," Harry went on. "She had a couple of children fill two pint jars with water. They put one on the radiator cover, where it is very warm, and one in the cold closet. Now they're waiting to see what happens."

"Those kids are learning the same kinds of things we're getting in our environmental science class *here:* evaporation!" Fred was indignant.

Rosemary's response was immediate. "But we're learning that stuff to be teacher aides. That's *different.*"

"Student teachers do go through many of the same experiences children do," I put in. "It helps them in their teaching." I didn't add that the PEC students were also learning for themselves as well, thinking to myself, You could have known much of it before you came here if, as young children, you had the same kinds of teachers you are presently working with in the nursery schools.

Indeed, this problem solving the PEC students are exposed to, as they observe and help in their fieldwork placements, is deceptively simple on the surface; taking in, as it does, the concepts of quantity, size, sequence, comparison, and a host of other ideas, it is the kind of experiencing that is essential to cognitive development.

CATCHING UP ON LOST SKILLS

The *obvious* indifference most MLD display about their learning problems usually stems from their feelings of incompetence and the accompanying embarrassment. Often the root of their trouble is not apparent; this was illustrated by Dina shortly after she entered the program. She was a reliable, conscientious, helpful student, both in the PEC course work, and in her fieldwork placement, yet she did not follow the rule of calling her cooperating teacher ahead if she was going to be absent or excessively tardy. In her case, the neglect was conspicuous, for her father's illness took her away from her responsibilities more often than is normal, and on some occasions when her presence was most essential.

For the third time in two weeks, Dina's PEC fieldwork supervisor, who was also her tutor, had to call her to task:

"You knew the class was going on a trip the first thing Wednesday morning and that if you weren't there, Mr. Welch would have to get someone else in your place?"

"Yes."

"Did you *think* of telephoning?"

"Yes."

"I *know* you've got the number."

"Yes. But I don't know where I put it. Everything is so crazy at home."

"I understand that very well. But why didn't you look in the telephone book?"

Silence, as Dina fussed with her books.

The light dawned on her tutor. "You don't know how?"

"No."

"And you don't know how to ask the operator?"

"No."

"How did you expect to get through the school year this way?"

"I don't know."

"Don't you want to know how?"

"Yes, it's hard not to know."

"You must ask. You know how much we want to help you."

"I was ashamed." Tears streamed down Dina's face.

However hard the experience was for her, it pushed Dina into the details of the use of the dictionary, as she worked on alphabetization, spelling, syllabication, and other matters relating to her reading problems, a few of which had already emerged, as she worked with her tutor on her homework and daily child study logs.

As with all of these lost or weak skills, there are many

aspects to the problem, and her tutor had her work on them for at least twenty minutes during their once-a-week sessions throughout the two years she was in the PEC Program.

Constant practice and repetition are mandatory, if the improvement is to be permanent. Even so, as Dina got more competent, it became clear that she would never be skillful in looking up words, but she did learn to manage when it was necessary, to her own great satisfaction. In fact, she went about boasting of her newfound ability to use the phone book—an endearing, childlike quality so many of our students show, and one that seems incongruous, considering the shame and fear that often cover up disability.

Another common problem which our young adults could have solved as children, had they had suitable assistance, emerged in the case of Berta, several days after she began working in the nursery school. Berta brought her own lunch and ate it with the nursery school teachers—a not infrequent arrangement in the smaller setups, where there is no kitchen. Berta's general appearance, and her overall performance, gave no clue whatsoever to one of her problems, as the three teachers sent her out for their daily sandwiches.

Resourceful in covering up, the way most MLD usually are, Berta carried the three amounts of money in her bag and two of her pockets, paying the cashier separately from each one, and asking for separate amounts of change. The cashier made no secret of her annoyance, as the line behind Berta was held up each day. When Berta appeared for her tutoring session, she was a bundle of anxiety, and as she recounted the tale, she wept copiously.

It was to Berta's credit that she could acknowledge her difficulty, instead of trying to circumnavigate it, as other students in analogous situations have done, concocting flimsy excuses to get a change of placement, or suffering along until a teacher discovered the trouble.

"How have you managed the bus or subway all of these years?" her tutor asked, reaching for the money box.

"My parents take me, or they give me the exact change."

"Well, let's start practicing right now. Meanwhile tell your school to give you the exact change until you get the hang of it; or let me tell them if you find it too hard."

In addition to the practice with money in the tutoring hour, Berta was given written homework assignments that involved the many kinds of money problems she was likely to be confronted with; and, at the end of six weeks, with about fifteen minutes' practice each session, Berta was pleased to tell her school that making change was no longer a problem to her.

The MLD's trouble in telling the exact time—something common to many of them—usually emerges early in the PEC Program. All of the students can read the hour and half hour, but some have trouble with the minutes and seconds in between; they also get confused with the mixture of "to," "before," or "of," in comprehending the last half-hour's reading. Then there are students who have difficulty planning around the clock, even when they can read it; frequently I have found that these are students who have no regular set schedule or routine. In any case, one way the clock difficulty reveals itself is when the student is constantly late, but claims "the train keeps breaking down"; or, "I left in plenty of time," as Oscar told me. "I can't see why I should be late."

"What's plenty of time?" I asked Oscar.

"Two hours."

"But you only live forty-five minutes away."

A blank stare.

"What time do you leave in the morning?"

"Seven thirty."

"What's an hour from then?"

"Eight thirty."

"What's forty-five minutes?"

Silence.

"Look at the clock on the wall. What time is it now?"

"Nine thirty."

"No, it's thirty-eight minutes after nine. Do you have difficulty reading time?"

"Not really."

"Could it be that that's why you're late so often?"

"I don't think so."

"Well, check it out with your tutor. If you do, you ought to get it straightened out right away."

As is sometimes the case, Oscar said nothing to his tutor, but I immediately passed the word along so that she took up his tardiness when she next saw him. Afterward, in reporting back about it, she said, "Oscar's school says he can't be more helpful; apparently, if the clock problem shows up there, they are not yet aware of it. But the thing that beats me is how blithely he insists he can read the clock at the same time that he has read it wrong." Sympathetic, as the tutors always are, she added, "I guess it's just too hard for him to face."

BUT WISDOM IS THERE

Many of our PEC students, who are alert to the ways of children, can learn a great deal about themselves, even though they may not always realize it; they can also show a great deal of wisdom.

Not long after school opened in the fall, a new student, Riva, asked in child study, "Why does Johnny in my class always follow me around?"

One student said, "Maybe he's lonely."

Another: "Maybe he likes you."

A third: "Maybe he doesn't get enough attention at home."

Grace said, "Maybe he's got a new baby sister or brother."

"He might be afraid?" Dale ventured.

"Those are all good answers," I put in. "Let's suppose any one of them is true. What's the best way to help the boy? We've already talked about 'social development' a number of times."

"Get him to play with other children," Gene said.

"How do you do that?"

"Take him over where other children are busy and ask them to let him play," came from Dale again.

"Have you tried that, Riva? It's a good suggestion."

"No." She grinned.

"Do you like Johnny to follow you around?"

"Wellll." More grinning.

"Do you encourage it?"

"What does 'encourage' mean?"

"Do you go out of your way to be nice to him? Do you bring him candy or pamper him?"

"Well, I do pay extra attention to him."

"Do you *need* him to follow you around?"

A grin and no answer.

"Has your teacher asked you to give him extra attention?"

"She asked me *not* to."

"Gee, Riva," Elaine was deadly earnest, "he can't spend the rest of his life following grown-up people around. Why don't you listen to your teacher?"

I turned to another subject, knowing that Riva got the point.

THE HOMEWORK OF THE STUDENT WHO RAISED THE QUESTION OF WHY A CHILD IN HER CLASS ALWAYS FOLLOWS HER AROUND. THIS WAS WRITTEN BEFORE PEC ADOPTED PRINTING FOR THE PURPOSES OF READING AND WRITING.

Why Johnny Tagged After the Assitant Teacher

Johnny might have felt that his parents ~~or weren't~~ weren't showing him enough love or affection. So Johnny might have felt secure if he stayed by his student teacher. He might have felt that she would understand Johnny's ~~problem~~. Another reason Johnny might off [have] tagged after his student teacher, was maybe he didn't feel comfortable with the other children. I would try to get Johnny interested in doing something ~~that~~ he might like to do such as draw, paint, tell him that ~~the~~ other children want him to be ~~h~~ his friends and try to get him to play with the other children.

At another time, Gerta, a new student, opened with, "We've got a five-year-old brat who is always saying dirty words—words that begin with *f* and *sh* you-know-what. It's disgusting. I'd like to smack him."

Second-year Raymond's response was strong. "Look, Gerta, you're a teacher aide, not another five-year-old; and he isn't a brat."

"Well yesterday he told me to 'shut up.' "

"Yeah," from Diane. "I've got a couple in my school like that."

"Does your five-year-old play with the other children, Gerta?" I asked.

"Not much. He hangs around them, knocks down their blocks, and gets into fights."

"What does your teacher do?" Adelaid asked.

"Mrs. Wilsen tells him, 'Larry, we don't talk that way here,' but she doesn't get mad at him."

"Where do you suppose he learns those words?" I asked.

There were several guesses: "From other children?"

"From his parents?"

"From a sister or brother?"

"Possibly. When do we adults swear?"

There were various answers: "When we're mad."

"When we don't like someone."

"When we're hurt."

"To get rid of feeling."

"Do you suppose a five-year-old means the same things when he says those words as an adult does?"

"Well, the other children might start copying him," Wayne spoke up.

I turned to Wilma. "Can you think of anything Miss Wilsen does that helps?"

"Well, yesterday she sat him down next to her and read him a story."

"She diverted him!" Vincent was enthusiastically referring to an idea I had introduced a few weeks back.

"Yes; she got him interested in the story," from Bernice.

"Always the best key," I added. "It helps him to get into another mood."

"My father swore a lot," Bill chimed in. "Once he yelled at me when I said 'Hell' and I said, 'You swear.' "

"What did he do?" from Sheldon.

"He looked at me, and said, 'I guess I do. I never thought about it.' "

"He was honest!" Claudia exclaimed.

"Parents don't always realize that sometimes children copy adults," I added.

"Maybe if Miss Wilsen talked to Larry's parents it would help?" Wilma asked.

"She probably will if she hasn't already, Wilma."

"But you've got to be able to know what to do with him in school. Understanding sure helps."

"That's right, Raymond." I could see why his school thought so highly of him.

"I have a child, Adam, who always wants to be held in the teacher's lap," Percy said, during a child study class. "I'm with four-year-olds."

A couple of students had immediate ideas.

"He's lonely."

"Maybe he's spoiled."

"What is it to be spoiled?" I asked.

"Too much love?"

"Is too much food good for a child?" I questioned in return.

"He gets fat," from Gerald.

Bruce, who hardly ever spoke up: "Fat people are weaker."

Why [does] dose a child use bad language?

He use bad language because he
may be angry or he may
just want to try it out and see
what the parent will say.
He may [heard] here a parent or an
other child use the talk.

Why do we [get angry] garnry When a child
swears?
Our feeling[s] are hurt — we
think it is a [personal] perial attack.
We think the child knows the
really [really] meaning of the word."
We get [embarrassed] smassart, [because] because
if we are parent[s] we don't
want other people to think
we talk that way at home or
he learned at home.

"That's a thoughtful point, Bruce; whatever brought that to your mind?"

"My brother's fat. He weighs a ton."

"Well, what's that got to do with too much love?"

"It makes a child weaker," Robin said.

"How?"

Bruce again: "He expects it every minute so he can't stand up for himself."

"So 'spoiled' isn't any favor?"

"A rotten apple is spoiled," Tina called out.

"What other reasons might Adam always want to sit on the teacher's lap?"

"Maybe he's got a new brother or sister?"

"Possibly."

"Maybe his parents just got separated or divorced," Lance suggested.

Olive said, "I think it's much harder for the child if the parents are divorced than if one dies."

There were gasps. The class was obviously shocked; I sat and listened to the vehement disagreements.

"You're crazy."

"You don't know what you are talking about."

"Death is the worst thing in the world."

"If you lost your father when you were young the way I did, you'd know better than to say that."

Olive's voice shook as she responded: "Well, my parents were divorced when I was nine. This way your father's alive and he's here, but he doesn't want you even when you want him so much it hurts."

Plaintively from a student: "Not all divorces are that bad, are they, Dr. Kranes?"

"There's no ruler to measure. It depends on the situation. Death is terribly painful, and so is divorce. We can all argue all about it. But let's get back to Adam." I knew it was time to leave the controversy.

Without looking at the job chart I could tell who put the place mats out. It was Paddy (5½) because he put his best friends and himself at the round table where no teacher sits.

We, were doing the "Ch" sound in reading readiness and the children had to draw 4 pictures with words beginning with it, so Jean-Christophe said he was going to draw a potato chip, so the other 3 boys at the table did the same thing. It was the first time Jean-C started something and the others followed.

"We can help him even when we don't know the reason," Phillip said.

I closed with, "That's what all good teachers do." And I thought to myself, You students may have your learning problems but wisdom is there.

7

PEC
Young Adult Problems
and
More Implications

A CAMERA VIEW

The majority of visitors who observe our MLD students, most of whom have worked with the more extreme learning disabled, tell us that "they appear normal," and that they can see "nothing wrong with them"; that they "look and sound like any college student." One important professional who works in a program for a more learning-disabled population, upon observing not long ago, said, in a disconcerting moment, "Their problems are emotional; you can see it in their eyes."

The comment reminded me of my first efforts, in 1964, to develop a program for the MLD, when I ran about frantically, trying to connect with some educators in special education, who, knowing more than I, might provide some guidance. One professor, in a ten-minute meeting, suggested that I return with a fully detailed document of my hypothesis, future plans, and so on; I spent many anxious hours fulfilling his request. But when I appeared for our next meeting, he was not present, nor, said his secretary, was there any sign on his calendar about me. I left my telephone number, but he never called.

Some half-dozen years later, an educator interested in the field did consent to act as a PEC part-time consultant for a year, saying, however, "The reason no one ever responded to you is because none of us know anything at all about your population, or how to work with them; I'll come, but it will be to learn."

Well, we know much more now than we did then, but we've just scraped the surface. The reason, in part, is that, generally speaking, the MLD's problems are usually so muted. If our young adults were hyperactive, distractible, and impulsive as children, and some of the parents report that they were, these signs have largely disappeared; if they are seizure prone, it is well under control; if some of the students have an ungainly gait, a flat walk, or poorish coordination, these traits are not usually more obvious than one sees in some of the population-at-large.

In order to qualify for the PEC Program, our students must be well-mannered, neat, well-spoken, and reasonably well put together. They come from all backgrounds —from the disadvantaged to the wealthy. At a staff meeting recently, our group counselor said, "Its extraordinary how you can take students so different from each other and mold them into a unified whole." I suppose it is because of the common goal—their desire to be a teacher aide. At any rate, we occasionally get students who show no perceptual or any neurological dysfunction that we, or his medical examinations, have been able to detect. Usually this type of student comes from the disadvantaged group. By the time such students graduate, we have decided that their learning difficulties are the result of their long years of deprivation, and not from any organic dysfunction.

Our admission requirements, although firm, are flexible; we may overlook any one of them, if the applicant appears to have unusually good potential, and if we have his parents' cooperation. But we're even weak-kneed, at times, in that regard, although we should have learned, by this time, that if a student comes with some extreme problems, and we cannot turn to the parents for support, we are, more often than not, doomed to fail.

Some literature about the "slow-learner" child indicates that he often looks several years younger than he is. This is usually true of our young adult women, but oddly enough, it has not been true of our male population. I have had no way of determining whether this is happenstance, or based upon something more substantial.

All of the PEC students need much more help in their learning processes than the regular student; this, in addition to their more intense personality problems, common to most of them, prescribes that young adult classes contain not more than fifteen students, and preferably not more than twelve.

In a group, and without supervision, a few are likely to become loud and silly, although, as our society grows less inhibited these days, I'm not sure they now stand out as much in this regard. Still, there is no doubt that, in an unfavorable climate, the self-imposed restraints of some are likely to fall away rather quickly, particularly in a permissive society. In fact, almost all of the MLD are far better off in a structured setting with caring, sympathetic, supportive figures of authority, who provide guidelines.

My own puzzlement, as I began working with the MLD, was very great. Taken in by their usual verbal fluency, I at first concluded—wrongly—that their learning problems grew out of an emotional instability, instead of the other way around. But I soon realized that the perceptual problems so common to the PEC young adults, and their difficulties in abstracting and integrating complexities, were not typical of my previous regular school students.

Another marked difference is that most MLD tend to generalize in the broadest manner, paying very little attention to specifics; also, generally, their written expression is notably constrained, even if the student is at the uppermost level of the 75 to 95 IQ range, and no matter how verbally articulate. It's almost as if, in recording a thought, these students are ploddingly recording a new language. Without exception, the written work of our PEC young adults never does justice to their thinking capacity.

Yet, with all of their cognitive difficulties, it is the rare MLD who is not extremely sensitive to others' feelings; and often those not on the highest end of the IQ scale come up with astonishingly good insights and amazingly wise propositions, when the subject relates in some way to the human condition. According to a number of cooperating schoolteachers, some are more reliable, conscientious, and devoted than the regular paid assistant; and there are those who do better with children. Be that as it may, there are always problems, just as there are in the training of regular university students who prepare for a profession.

THE MISPLACED STUDENT

For one thing, as effective as we find our screening procedures, one of the inevitable difficulties is the occasional misplaced student. As agonizing as the decision is to have to redirect an unfortunate student like this, in some ways the decision should be relatively simple; yet, I suppose, nothing can be simple when it involves human error, shattered wishes, and soft hearts that fret over the possibility of being unfair.

Some of the trauma lies in the timing of the final resolution to redirect the student. After an orientation period, the novice is put in a carefully chosen fieldwork placement, where, one might expect, his ability to relate well to children could be quickly determined, particularly with the cooperating teacher's constant presence, and the regular and frequent visits from the student's PEC supervisor. But there are never-ending questions: Is the student not doing well because, new, he is fearful and nervous? Because he is afraid of his cooperating teacher or his PEC supervisor? Is he getting too little guidance from an overworked head teacher? Or not enough of a chance to function? Should he be with a different age level?

Then there may be the complication of someone on the PEC staff, possibly the cooperating teacher, over-identifying with the trainee, going overboard, unconsciously, to postpone the painful decision. The student must have every chance to succeed, and as we review the situation, over half of the first term has passed us by. Fortunately, the dangers of moving in too fast, or too soon, are well-appreciated by most parents; at any rate, though, in a critical situation, it takes wise and strong leadership to bring it to a point of decision. Sometimes there are strong feelings to encounter no matter how farsighted the decision is; but the fair, objective attitude, sooner or later, wins.

One might expect that the misplaced student's discomfort would be so great that he would want "out." Yet, most of the time this is not the case; in fact, it is more frequently the able student, who, upon some error in judgment in his work with the children, will feel inadequate and offer to quit.

Another interesting angle is that, occasionally, in redirecting a student, we find that it was the parents' desire that the child be a teacher aide, which the uncertain child grabbed onto; nevertheless that does not miff us. PEC young adults, like so many youngsters these days, usually are very uncertain of their direction; frequently they need a push from their parents, and if they have the talent, as is most always the case, when they decide to come, they are successful graduates.

THE HIDDEN HANDICAP
UNDERGROUND

There is another category of difficulty: the able but overprotected child who doesn't usually make it at PEC unless his parents are completely supportive of the program. Ironically, the very nature of this problem inhibits the parents from accepting our position.

Ralph belonged to this group. Among his recommendations was one from a camp for exceptional children, where he had been an aide to a counselor. The camp director wrote: "Ralph has done a very good job this summer. He is a lot of fun, and the children and counselors take to him easily, but we are not sure how well he will do in a more demanding situation."

Ralph's academic standing was at the top of the 75 to 95 IQ range; he was quite handsome, well-groomed, obviously charming, and more sophisticated on the surface than most of our PEC students. Besides jogging every day, he was greatly interested in sports, particularly baseball, playing on the neighborhood team. Still, his physical coordination and skills were not on a high enough level for him to build a career as an athlete in the field; nor would his learning disabilities allow him to earn a degree in physical education. Actually, he had worked as a field hand one summer at a regular sports camp for non-learning disabled children, but he found it "boring" and nothing came of it.

From Ralph's external behavior, there were no signs of his learning disabilities. In social situations, he was adept at using his interest and knowledge of the sports world to cover up his superficiality, and lack of focus, generally; but to say that is to ignore his reasonably good comprehension in reading and elementary math, although he did show many perceptual problems in his written work and a marked disability in expressing ideas in writing. Whenever he put forth any concerted effort, however, no matter what the subject was, there was decided improvement. The trouble was that Ralph did not seem to know what hard work meant. Largely, in his PEC classes, he horsed around, calling attention to himself, borrowing supplies he kept forgetting to bring to class, making wisecracks on the side during discussions, and constantly leaving the room; if anything, he was a demoralizing influence on the other students, particularly because they found him unusually attractive.

As the PEC work grew in difficulty, Ralph's learning problems became more apparent, and so did his lack of effort. Mainly, he used his interest in sports and jogging as an excuse for undone homework; then, as more pressure was brought to bear on him, he began calling the program "baby stuff," and "boring." While his cooperating school found him "attractive and relating nicely to children," their report went on to say that "he is often not where he is supposed to be when we need him. He hangs around the assistant teachers when they have time off, or he will be running errands for someone in the office."

Ralph's consistently unresponsive attitude toward his PEC supervisor's efforts to discuss what was going on, along with his negative effect on the other students, led us to decide to ask his parents in for a meeting. They were an attractive, urbane couple; when we called them, they seemed very eager to come. But they were hardly seated when we were informed by Mrs. Zan that, "Ralph, you know, is a very good boy at home."

"Yes," from her husband. "We were about to call *you*, but you beat us to it. I guess you know that Ralph is bored—not surprising for your top student, I guess."

As gently as we could, Ralph's supervisor and I drew the true picture of his faltering adjustment in the program, presenting his strengths, but not glossing over his weaknesses.

Both parents expressed amazement. Mrs. Zan led off with, "He was the best student at the _____ School [the record didn't support her claim], and the most popular."

The father continued: "We have put a lifetime into helping Ralph in his sports, and, more recently, into jogging; none of that part of his life should be undermined."

Agreeing fully that their son's athletic inclinations were all to the positive, we, nevertheless, indicated how his routine and schedule could be shaped to accommodate both his sports interests and his PEC work; we also emphasized that, whether it was this profession, or in another area, Ralph was of an age where he would have to settle down and work hard if he was to be at all successful.

The Zans were obviously sobered; they expressed the desire to cooperate, and agreed that their son should receive weekly professional counseling, "although," said his mother, "he was in therapy a few years ago and it was useless. He is not nervous, as you know, and he has lots of confidence. All he has to do is to make up his mind to buckle down to work."

Neither the supervisor nor I made any response, but, instead, with Ralph's parents, decided what approach should be made to their son in reporting about his parents' and our meeting together. With that done, we wished his mother and father well as they departed.

Ralph began to work hard, after we saw the Zans, and at the same time he went into counseling. Unfortunately, from what we could gather, about that same time he became enamored of an assistant teacher in his co-operating school, with what seemed to be her encouragement. Soon his head teacher reported, "He is making a pest of himself." The next thing we knew, he dropped out of therapy. Ralph's supervisor and I then decided that I should try a meeting with Ralph, alone, in my office.

"Hi," he greeted me, seating himself on the chair opposite, crossing one leg over the other. "This is a nice office."

"It's a nice place altogether; don't you think so?"

"Yep."

"How are you liking your PEC work?"

"OK; but it's too easy; it's boring."

"But you don't hand in your work half the time."

"It bores me."

"Maybe if you dug at it harder, you might find more things to interest you. You need more practice expressing your ideas in writing, too, Ralph."

"Yeah, but my jogging and baseball keep me terribly busy."

"Well, I guess you are not as interested in working with children as we thought."

"I am, and I get along fine with them."

"But you can't be a teacher aide without passing your course work."

"But I'm good with children without PEC. Even the nursery school says so."

"There are lots of ways of being good with children. You're a natural with them, Ralph, but if you learned more here, you would do much better."

"How come?"

"It's a little like being a farmer; you can plant things with a little knowledge and they grow. But the more you understand about the soil, rainfall, weather, and other things, the better fruit you'll get."

"OK. But I don't understand why I have to keep going to a headshrink."

"To help you understand why you do things like going on errands when you should be with the children in your classroom and a lot of other things that spoil your ability. You're wasting it."

"I'll have to talk it over with my parents. I don't need a headshrink to help me not go on errands."

"It's a good idea to talk it over with your parents. I think the three of us should meet here again. Would you be willing?"

"Sure thing."

But the next time we called the Zans for an appointment, Ralph's mother said, "We think we've done enough talking. Ralph finds the program is too boring. He'll finish this week and that's it."

Ralph had very good possibilities and we were sorry he did not work out. Within our experience, unhappily, among our high level MLD, some who can easily pass for the non-learning disabled, are often the most lost and depressed in the student group. Yet, who won't cover up a deficit that hardly shows? The trouble is that unless the problem is confronted, the wounds it causes can't be healed. Acknowledging the disability frees the parents and child to move ahead in the pursuit of worthwhile objectives.

A STUDENT MANAGES

Andrea Morrow belonged to another group whose problems might have profited from counseling, but who managed to succeed on her own. She was an attractive applicant, and her responses in the screening session were impressive, yet, obviously, she had a chip on her shoulder, and she was negative and sullen.

But Andrea's parents were reassuring in the empathy and understanding that they showed toward their daughter. They believed that because of Andrea's dyslexic problems, in addition to her other learning difficulties, the schools had shortchanged her. "She was so bogged down with the errors in her homework that she never got a chance to show her intelligence," Mrs. Morrow explained.

"So," added her father, "you see a resentful, miserable soul."

But Mrs. Morrow was cheerful. "She simply loves children. Even when the _____ School dropped her, they said she was the best helper in their kindergarten. Then, when my sister was in the hospital this spring, Andrea took over almost the whole responsibility for her four-year-old little girl. Her common sense and good judgment were amazing."

"Like my wife," Mr. Morrow smiled. "It's too bad that girl has gotten so bitter. She says she will do anything rather than go back to school."

"That's right," his wife broke in quickly, "but really, Andy, she did agree to try this last time." Then turning to me: "We promised her that if it didn't work out, she wouldn't have to finish the year."

Andrea's overall IQ score was 89 when she came into the program; retested just before she graduated, it was 103, with her verbal score moving from 91 to 97, and her performance from 89 to 111. She was a very hard worker, and her spelling and writing improved considerably. She was also a leader in class discussions.

In her fieldwork Andrea was very reliable with children, showed wisdom and good judgment, but she was temperamental, and too easily felt that she was being taken advantage of. Nevertheless, Miss Rich, her cooperating teacher, said she was as good as any paid assistant, and better than some. "After all," she mused, "which one of us doesn't have some personality quirks?"

Then came a new wrinkle. Andrea was having trouble with the paid assistant, Lorraine, of whom, her PEC supervisor said, she was very envious. Lorraine was Andrea's head teacher whenever Miss Rich was absent. During those times, Andrea responded to Lorraine with insolence and disrespect.

When, as occasionally happens, our MLD students in training know as much as, or more than, the paid assistant does about school procedures, the envy of the aide is much more difficult to handle. I expected Andrea to be impossible. But she appeared cheerfully enough in my office until I told her the reason I had called her in; then the smile froze on her face.

"Who told you?"

"Miss Rich. They can't put up with that kind of behavior."

"Don't worry; I'm not that way with the children."

"If you can't get along with your head teachers, you won't be able to work with children."

"Why should I take orders from Lorraine? I know more than she does."

"In some ways maybe you do. Lots of us know more, sometimes, than the people we work under."

"That's rotten! It's unfair!"

"Lots of things in life are unfair. I put up with things I don't like, too. But if the job's worth it, you have to overlook them."

Scornfully: "You! You put up with things? That's a big fat joke. What would *you* ever have to put up with? Everyone knows you're the big boss."

"You'll have to learn how to put up with Lorraine, Andrea."

"Well you can bet your life I won't. She's too damned big for her breeches!" And with that, Andrea bolted from her chair, yelling, "I'm quitting this stinking program," and stalked out.

Andrea will just have to get some counseling, I wearily thought, as I prepared to see a student for tutoring. I'll have to call her parents tomorrow. But I no sooner got to the office the next morning when Andrea was on the phone.

"I'm sorry, Dr. Kranes. Can I come to see you later?"

"Let's wait for your tutoring hour tomorrow, Andrea, if that's all right with you. There's not enough time today for a good talk."

Andrea was all compunction the next day as she apologized. I asked her, "How about some counseling? It might make life easier for you."

"My parents suggested it last night. They are always suggesting it."

"Well?"

Pleadingly: "Can I have more time? I think I can work it out."

My hunch was that she could—even though there were two more crises shortly afterward: once when Andrea felt that she was doing much more housekeeping than Lorraine, and another time, when she had planned an activity that got postponed at the last minute because of an unexpected occurrence that changed the nursery school schedule. Both times, when we were discussing her show of temper toward Lorraine, Andrea stalked out of my office in the middle of the meeting, but both times she was back within a few moments.

Now, a few years later, when Andrea visits, we laugh about those events. I still remember the day she graduated. After the diplomas were handed out, she came up to me and said sweetly, "I *did* manage, didn't I?" She now works as a paid teacher aide in a day-care center and manages very well indeed.

COUNSELING HELPS

Roger Harkam was a student whose difficulties were amenable to therapy. Upon admission, his overall IQ was scored at 76. At graduation, it rose to 81, with the verbal moving from 77 to 80, and the performance from 78 to 86—no great rise, by any means, but, as in the case of a number of our students, his improvement outshone his scores.

To begin with, Roger was a natural with children, being tender and kind, but also firm; his work at PEC was another story, however. For, although he showed a reasonably good understanding of the courses, his papers were sloppily, and, it seemed, indifferently done; also they frequently came in late, and he was frequently absent from classes.

Roger's entire attitude with his tutor was, "I'm no good at academic work; what's the use of trying?" Unfortunately, his cooperating teacher, in her efforts to help him, erroneously supported his attitude, in that she emphasized his talents with children, playing down the scholastic area, where she knew he was having trouble. But she quickly got the point, once Roger's PEC adviser met with her.

Still, Roger was not amenable in the tutoring sessions. One day, upon being told, "You won't do better until you change your attitude," he grimaced. "If I can't be a teacher aide without the PEC courses, forget it." After two weeks, when he did not show up for his next sessions —although he did go to his fieldwork—we asked his parents to meet with us.

The Harkams seemed very intelligent, caring, and sensible. They agreed that Roger should have some counseling help and felt sure that he was so well motivated in his work with children that he would cooperate. "He'd do anything to stay in that school with the children," his mother said. "He's been worried stiff about this meeting, thinking he'd be asked to withdraw."

What unfolded from the counseling sessions, as we later learned from the Harkams, was of great significance in understanding what was going on in their son's mind.

"I knew better in my heart," Mrs. Harkam said, "but I wanted him to go on to get a regular college diploma more than anything in the world. Every once in a while I would say to him, 'When you get out of PEC, you can finish up at another university.' He and his father knew he couldn't do it. So, rather than risk another failure, he unconsciously dragged his feet in the PEC courses."

Roger's mother met with the counselor a number of times herself; understanding her own unreal wishes, and Roger's conundrum, she seemed gradually able to reassure Roger; a probable result was the improvement in his PEC course work.

After graduation, Roger was hired by the school that

trained him; he has been there, happily, it has seemed, for a year and a half. But the director called us one day to say that Roger was leaving at the end of the school year. "He wants to go to a junior college in West Virginia; I think it's a great mistake. If he decides to return—although I haven't told him this—we'll manage to take him back."

Roger's parents are hoping that their son will change his mind and not leave his job. Both parents, when we talked to them in our follow-up procedures, felt that Roger should have continued in counseling after he left PEC. Mr. Harkam was plainly worried:

"The therapist suggested that Roger continue, but we all felt so good about his progress and so did he. He does do very well on the job, the school says, but we think that his brother's going away to college last fall, and his outstanding scholastic success all along the way, has just been too much for Roger. He insists on trying again."

"Well, this try may at last settle him," I suggested, "and he can go back to his job if he wants to."

"In that case, back to counseling, too," was Mr. Harkam's response. "It did a lot for him. It relieves us to know that it's there."

SEX EDUCATION

Well-trained therapists, who have had experience working with MLD young adults, are hard to come by; early in PEC's history, however, I did find a traditionally trained psychiatrist, very warm and outgoing, who was willing to try counseling our students. Unfortunately, she knew next to nothing about the dynamics of the MLD's behavior, and at that early time, I felt hesitant to make any suggestions that might guide her. Deeply interested in group therapy, she felt that having a weekly session with all of the students at one time—there were then seven in total—would bring the best results.

Unfortunately, she was immediately confronted in the first session by Katy, who, although a very talented teacher aide, was extremely preoccupied with sex—the result, probably, of her sister's loose living. She had already been in trouble with the law, and Katy herself had recently gotten into some difficulty with a neighbor.

The psychiatrist, instead of viewing the subject of sex as everything relating to the character of the male and female, with the differences and similarities, loving, mating, and the consequent joys and sorrows, plunged immediately and solely into the subject of sexual intercourse, bringing into the second session illustrations from a book that explicitly portrayed it.

The students, completely overwhelmed by this candid presentation, came to their PEC courses the following day, highly agitated, whispering and carrying on like very young children in possession of a wicked and poisonous secret. One of the students came into my office and wept. Needless to say, it took more than a little doing to calm them and their parents down. Since the psychiatrist's response to all of this was, "It's your and the parents' problem, not the students'," the counseling was discontinued.

The episode reminded me of my own experience in teaching a "sex course" to a class of ten-year-olds in a private school; besides giving me a lot of food for thought, it also taught me a valuable lesson—one that is relevant here, and worth recounting.

The parents in that particular school, highly educated and sophisticated as they were, felt squeamish about teaching their children the "facts of life." Hence, at a parents' meeting, they asked if some of the staff would work out a *modus operandi* for handling the subject. Being in the forefront of the experimental movement, the teachers decided to try the subject in a formal way. After some discussions, it was decided that the age of ten —"not too young, and not too old"—was the best period for the age of "enlightenment"; and since I then taught that age group, I was "it."

My instinct led me to use a gradual approach, beginning with the breeding of the one-celled amoeba, and working my way up to mating and breeding of the mammal; moving slowly over the year, we ended with the sexual act and reproduction.

At some points, especially when I would use the proper names of the sexual anatomy, the class would giggle in a silly fashion; then I would stop and tell them if they wanted to act like babies, they weren't ready to go on with this serious subject. That would immediately have them sitting up straight as ramrods.

At the end of the term, as was the usual custom, several classes, including ours, went to "June School," in the country, where we ended the year—a rich and valuable experience, albeit a tough one for staff members like me, who do not like to rough it.

It was a very primitive situation for a modern school setting. The bunks, containing eight cots each, were strung out in henhouse fashion, with short partitions between them, connected by a long aisle running along the length of the largely open building. The teacher's room at the front was the only one that had a partition running to the ceiling; the wall was full of knotholes.

Undressing to go to bed, the first night, I heard shuffling and giggling on the other side of my partition, which faced the children's first bunk. Throwing on my robe, I quickly ran around to the other side, to find the

children had been stacked up on four of the beds, peek-
ing through the knotholes; they were trying to unscramble themselves as I emerged.

In high indignation (I was too surprised myself to act
reasonably), I scolded and punished them: no story hour
before bedtime the next night, with curfew one hour
earlier; and from then on I undressed in a corner where
I knew that they would not be able to see me. Other than
that, I dismissed the incident—that is, until the next
one.

A few days later, I went to take a shower at my usual
hour. The water contraption, a narrow kind of closet,
lined with galvanized tin, was open to the sky at the top.
As I soaped myself, reveling in the only hot water at
camp, I heard scrambling on the outside walls, and upon
looking up, saw signs of three children attempting to
hang over the top. My anger, this time, contained an
overwhelming sense of disappointment.

As soon as I could, I asked to meet with the newly
appointed school psychologist, who, as luck would have
it, had come to spend the weekend with us at camp.

"Why," I asked, in my first question, "if they have
learned all about sex, do they behave that way?"

Dr. Wayne explained: "No one, not even adults, can
know 'all about sex'; like the subject of death, it is one of
the profoundest mysteries of life.

"Too great an exposure to sex is as stimulating as trying
to bury the subject; like everything else, one takes it in
gradually," she continued.

"Usually, very young children come to it through the
mother's pregnancy, or the birth of a sibling; but when a
child of three says, 'My mother's got a baby in her stomach; how did it get there?' his question does not require
the same kind of answer as a youngster of ten does—not
that the older child is likely to raise the question aloud
either.

Having taught nursery school ages for a few years after that, I learned how right Dr. Wayne was. With the child's question or comment, I would hardly have the response out of my mouth before he would be off, interested in something else. For example, during snack time, four-year-old Abigail asked, drinking her orange juice, "How did the baby get in Mommy's stomach?"

"Your daddy planted the seed," I said.

Abigail's response was, "Could I have some more orange juice?"

Or one morning as the fives were removing their wraps, Steve was telling in great excitement, "I've got a new puppy dog."

Myrna: "Did you know my mommy has a baby in her stomach and I can feel it?"

"Yes, you can feel it move," I agreed. "It's in a very special place."

But Myrna's attention was already elsewhere. Moving toward the housekeeping corner, she asked, "Where's Topsy?" (the childrens' favorite doll).

The child's interests, at this stage of his life, are too narrowly focused for him to linger long over such recondite matters. But for the older child, about age ten or eleven and up, some excellent books have been written on the subject. Parents could leave them lying around the house for the child to read, as his interest moves him. If the child feels free to ask questions in the preceding years, or later, so much the better. At any rate, it is the rare youngster who doesn't get some enlightenment from other sources, with, usually, a little experience. That's only natural. Sex is an integral part of life, and not something to be learned through formal lessons in the elementary-school years.

THE DYNAMICS OF THE MLD'S BEHAVIOR

The question of the dynamics of the MLD's behavior puzzles most of us who work with them. Much of the information in this area deals with younger children who have normal or above normal IQs, but who have severe dyslexic problems; or with those individuals—the retarded—whose IQs are markedly below the MLD's, or with the "brain damaged," many of whom probably belong to the MLD population. A large number of all of these people, as young children, are described as having difficulties in social perception as a result of their neurological problems. There seems to be general agreement that they often become capable of understanding some things at a later chronological age than the non-learning disabled, and that as very young children, they need to be trained and drilled in certain social situations to help them learn how to behave appropriately.

There are medical authorities, though, including Dr. Eisenberg, and some psychologists, like Dr. Sarason, who theorize that much of the difficult behavior connected with the brain-damage syndrome is the result *not* of the organic defect, but of the psychological blows society heaps upon them. They contend that without the cultural assaults, the learning disabled would function with fewer emotional difficulties. I have come to share this point of view. For one thing, among the approximately 50 percent of our young adult population who live in a residence, the students who have the greatest personal and social problems are often the most able in the cognitive areas.

Those who work with our MLD and do not share my perspective might theorize that the neurological impairment impedes the individual's understanding of cause and effect. They suspected, for instance, that, when one of our students deliberately went off to a small town with a man she didn't know, the girl was completely unaware of her responsibility and unable to take in the consequences of her behavior.

The student in question was below the median of our IQ range. Still, she had no difficulty in realizing her responsibilities in connection with the PEC Program, and in her work with children, their parents or teachers, or her own peers. Besides, other PEC students whose scores were on a par with hers, whatever their cognitive problems, were shocked at the young lady's behavior; in fact they took it upon themselves to try to help guide her. But this young adult behaved as if she would not be guided in *this* situation. She showed a concentrated desire to enter into an "affair"—something, we later learned, that was apparent before she became a PEC student. One can only surmise the reason, but in my judgment this student's intense wish propelled her behavior. Emotion winning over good judgment—a not uncommon occurrence with many people.

PEC therapists are meticulous, of course, in not sharing any of their counselees' or their parents' confidences; at the same time all of them know that the PEC staff keeps the counselor informed of difficulties the students present in the program that negatively affect their performance. Among such problems are consistent tardiness and absences, low-level frustration that interferes with work and relationships, consistent unreliability, inconsistent behavior, and depression.

The counselors, while being well-trained in traditional methods of therapy, work with the PEC students through their everyday practical problems, believing that, usually, this population is too vulnerable for deep probing into the psyche.

At best, most troubled MLD have great difficulty discussing their personal feelings on more than a superficial level, and they tend to complain in a repetitive fashion. Overattached to their parents, as many of them are, they, like the very young child, find it difficult not to blame them constantly. In fact, this very attachment often prevents them from creating a strong identity, and from being objective; they are unable to see their own responsibility in a troublesome situation of their own making. It is very rare for the distressed MLD to say, "It's my fault." Or, "I was responsible."

The counselors vary their technique according to the MLD's needs. One, who has the largest number of PEC students in individual counseling, resorts to methods that are nonverbal when she finds a student who is too inhibited to communicate orally.

"I'll teach them to operate the self-service elevator, how to find their way in the neighborhood, how to use money, or sculpting. I'll use any technique that will open them up. I even sit on the floor with them if that will help."

The PEC Program recently instituted group therapy as a requirement for all of its students. There are five individuals in each group, with the same counselor for all of them. While it is too early to draw conclusions, the arrangement appears to offer relief to all involved.

Whatever the case may be, I am convinced that there is a far smaller relationship between the MLD's scores and their behavior problems than between their behavioral problems and parental expectations. This is not at all meant to denigrate the role of parents, most of whom have given everything they have in an effort to improve their offspring's lot. But in a society where acquisition and power illuminate life, the MLD falls in its shadow, much to the parents' despair.

THE FUTURE

Parents, naturally, are worried about the MLD's long-time future. All of the PEC graduates have developed considerably as human beings. Parents report that even those who went into jobs other than teacher-aide work are far more successful as a result of their PEC training; being much more confident, they relate better to others, follow directions better, and are more productive generally. This is not surprising, for there are rigorous requirements involved in PEC training: appropriate grooming, signing in and out on a daily attendance sheet, performing a variety of tasks responsibly and reliably, relating to various kinds of people—children, teachers, assistants, kitchen staff, janitorial help, and so on—and meeting with all kinds of evaluation.

Of the total number of graduates, approximately 70 percent—some of whom are married—are working in the helping professions with young children in nursery schools and Head Start, in the public schools under the Comprehensive Employment and Training Act (CETA), and in schools and centers for the handicapped. About 15 percent are working in unallied fields—as electricians, house painters, and gas station attendants; approximately 15 percent are married, and 25 percent of them have babies and are not working; and around 4 percent are unemployed, a few of whom quit their jobs to go back and try to succeed in some college courses. We have unfortunately lost track of about 1 percent.

There is great concern about how well the MLD can manage independently on their own. While at PEC, about half of our population live away from home, the majority residing at the Parkside, a nonsectarian residence for businesswomen, under the auspices of the Salvation Army. This is a beautifully run residence, having the necessary safeguards, yet allowing the freedom young adults need. A few of our male students, whose parents live in New York City's suburbs, have chosen to reside at the YMCA or YMHA. On very rare occasions we have had students who have chosen to live in individual rented quarters, but this has not proved to be the best situation.

Almost anything that can be said about the way our young adults cope with independent living is true about the majority of any population except that, generally, the MLD are more intense about everything. An ordinary quarrel takes on major proportions, with other students taking sides; or an unexpected illness—an appendectomy, well under control, for example—is reacted to as if it were an earthquake.

The students who have pronounced social difficulties before moving into Parkside have the greatest problems getting along there. But functioning in the program, and with the therapy that is required under those circumstances, the student's growth is usually substantial enough for him to remain at PEC. Generally, the degree of the individual's difficulties seems not to be tied up in any way to the degree of his learning problems; if anything, often the less able students seem to fare best.

Most of our people spend their time in groups with other PEC young adults. They are usually quite supportive of each other, but when someone has a crisis, they tend to be more supportive if they are not too deeply involved with that person. Their spare time is usually spent doing their PEC homework, visiting back and forth, looking at TV, listening to stereo, and going to the movies. Many attend the recreation program held at PEC on Saturdays, but those who are near enough tend to go home for the weekend.

Whatever the problems, unquestionably living away from home produces the most favorable results. Judging by the parents' reports, the students return home with a greater degree of self-confidence, much better able to cope with others, and in better humor. As one parent put it, "My daughter came back saying she *feels* grown up and she *is*."

Of course there is always the question of matrimony. "If I could get my child married, that might solve the problems." Or, conversely, "How can these MLD marry; they can just about manage to take care of themselves?" Others worry about what kind of person would choose to marry someone with these learning disabilities. And there's the futile dream of a few: "Maybe it needn't be known."

Currently a great deal of concern is being expressed openly about the "learning disabled" and marriage. Much of the literature appears to be about the retarded who are reaching puberty, with parents expressing their views about marriage, parenthood, and the issue of sterilization. Some of these expressions are in response to Dr. Sol Gordon, who is probably the most outspoken leader of the sexual rights of the handicapped. At the same time, Dr. Gordon is strong in his feeling that many people, learning disabled or not, should not have children. He bases some of his suggestions on a pamphlet, *Am I Parental Material?* In his presentation he states that when Ann Landers asked her readers if they would have children if they had it to do over again, of the more than thirty thousand who replied, 70 percent said no. He writes, "The fact of a disability *per se* should not be an impediment to having children; the pertinent factor is whether a disabled couple can provide the care and love a child needs."

Parents respond in a variety of ways, depending upon their beliefs, religious or otherwise, upon the nature of their children's problems, and the financial situation. Most of our MLD parents, who have discussed this with me, would like to see their offspring married—and as stated, about 15 percent are. But the subject of their having children seems to be a chilling matter to most of them.

When PEC graduates come back to visit, I ask how their life is different now that they are salaried workers in the helping professions. "How has your life changed since you graduated?" I asked one student recently. Although put in her own words, her answer was typical, as she grinned with obvious satisfaction. "I've got a job I love. They need me and they know I'm there. It's like I went from nobody to somebody."

The following illustrates the feelings of a PEC student as expressed at the graduation exercises in June 1977. It was written by the student herself:

Dr. Kranes, Dean Griffiths, Mrs. Anderson, parents and friends, fellow graduates:

Today as I look around me, three thoughts come to my mind. Like most graduates on graduation day they are: 1) my past and present feelings; 2) my achievements; 3) special thanks to parents and PEC and best wishes to my fellow graduates.

In my past I just sat in the class listening, but not really understanding what was being said by the teacher. Out of this, my feeling toward learning wasn't very much because I didn't know what learning was about. Since I was put in a program like this, I have gotten the special help I needed to learn in normal classes. My inner ambition is now to go on learning.

My achievements in this program have been learning to work with children, helping them gain physical, cognitive, social, emotional, and sensory experience at their young ages, in a professional manner. I now have become more confident within myself to be a part of many youngsters' lives, helping them learn what I learned here at PEC.

I would like to give special thanks to my foster parents for their eighteen years of love, faith, and understanding of me with my special needs in their home. Ma and Dad, I want you both to know that my past is over, my present is now, and in my future I will never forget what you have both done for me. There will always be a place in my heart for you wherever I go.

I would like to give a very special thanks to my nursery _____ Day Care Center staff for teaching me the many techniques in teaching children to learn. To the PEC staff many thanks for guiding me the right way for two years in the program. I hope that you have learned from me to improve and have more PEC Programs around the world like this.

Special thanks to Dr. Kranes for helping me and acknowledging to me my weak points in expressing myself to people; to Mrs. Conrad for helping me realize more the purpose of learning is not only the joy for oneself, but to help others learn what you already know. To Mrs. Brown—the tutoring you have given me has really helped me a lot and will benefit me in my life. Many thanks to the people I have not mentioned for the special interest they have taken within some part of my life.

Best wishes to the graduates: We have won our past with a long struggle because of our special disabilities. Knowing our special needs now, this program has helped us. Before there was not much hope for us to achieve in education. In the past there wasn't as much knowledge about the special learning needs of individuals, but now the doors are open for filling our needs, as well as those of others.

Remember, we are human beings, too, and have a part in this world to become someone. I would like to thank you for letting me share my thoughts with you on this day.

APPENDIX

Guidelines for Helping the Marginally Learning Disabled Child

MATERIALS AND EQUIPMENT

Appropriate materials and equipment are essential for physical, social, and mental development, as well as providing for the child's inner resources and a more pleasurable existence.

Some Valuable Materials and Equipment	Some Things the Child Can Learn from Their Use
Books	The child learns to be quiet as he listens to story reading and as he looks at pictures; to express ideas; to take turns at talking; learns about different things in life, such as animals, farm and city life, other families, trains, airplanes, the postman, and fireman.
Puzzles and matching games	Learns to observe different sizes and shapes; to fit pieces together; develops muscle, arm, finger, and hand con-

	trol; learns to work alone; to be patient, use judgment.
Crayons, brushes, paints	Develops physical control; explores different colors; creates different shapes, works alone; shares and expresses ideas.
Indoor blocks	Learns to use and control body movement; builds on ideas; senses weight and balance, number and shapes, as he realizes "bigger," "smaller," "more," and a "few," "first," "last," and so on. Learns to work alone and with others; develops ingenuity.
Large outdoor blocks	Learns to use and control body movement; builds on ideas; learns to work alone and with others; develops ingenuity.
Tricycles and carts	Learns to use and control body movements; to manage wheels and direction and space.
Miniature household items; dolls or small figures; dress-up clothes	Household play helps define the adult's and child's roles; extends the imagination; socialization with other children; shares ideas.
Musical instruments, such as bells, triangle, drum, cymbal	These provide different sounds and pitch, and a means for learning about timing and rhythm. With other children takes turns; works in unison.
Indoor modeling clay; outdoor sandbox	Learns to use and control body movement; explores texture; creates different shapes; builds on ideas; learns to share and cooperate if other children are involved in sandbox.

ROUTINE AND SCHEDULE

A regular routine and schedule are necessary for the child's stability and to help him have a sense of time, enabling him to anticipate, plan, and better remember things. These factors are most useful in the development of self-control.

In the home, the routine includes the events of getting the child up, bathing him, feeding, nap- and playtimes, and so on.

If the child goes to day-care or nursery school, the schedule and routine of events, depending on the age level, and whether it is a half- or whole-day session, may look something like this:

Schedule	*Routine of Events*
8:30– 9:00	Arrival
9:00– 9:15	Circle time to discuss day's activities
9:15–10:15	Indoor activities: paint, clay work, household play, and so on
10:15–10:35	Midmorning snack
10:35–11:35	Outdoor play
11:35–12:00	Wash up and story
12:00–12:30	Lunch
12:30– 1:30	Rest
1:30– 2:00	Alternate days: Music and rhythms; indoor activities Storytime Table work (usually for five-year-olds) involves activities in reading, writing, and number-readiness work
2:00– 2:45	Outdoor play
2:45– 3:00	Dismissal

SOURCES

The information in this list has been compiled from the following sources: *The Directory for Exceptional Children*, 8th edition, "ACLD Listing of Colleges/Universities," and the "National Directory of Programs for LD's." It is provided as a service for parents and professionals, but represents only a sampling of the available facilities. The colleges and centers have not been inspected and, therefore, are not necessarily endorsed by the Association for Children with Learning Disabilities. Further information can be obtained by contacting the sources provided.

J. Kathryn Sargent, *The Directory for Exceptional Children*, 8th ed., 1978 (a listing of educational and training facilities)

> Porter Sargent Publishers, Inc.
> 11 Beacon Street
> Boston, Mass. 02108

P. M. Fielding, ed., and Dr. John R. Moss, directory consultant, *A National Directory of Four Year Colleges, Two Year Colleges and Post High School Training Programs for Young People with Learning Disabilities*, 2nd ed., 1975

> Partners in Publishing Company
> P.O. Box 50347
> Tulsa, Okla. 73140

ACLD—colleges/universities that accept students with learning disabilities

> Association for Children with Learning Disabilities
> 4156 Library Road
> Pittsburgh, Pa. 15234

For schools for MLD under age eighteen contact your state office or the

National Association for Learning Disabilities
4156 Library Road
Pittsburgh, Pa. 15234

UNITED STATES LEARNING DISABILITY CENTERS FOR YOUNG ADULTS* AGES 18 AND ABOVE

Pages 228–254

* Compiled by the Calder Fellows, Pamela Goldberg and Yigal Joseph.

UNITED STATES LEARNING DISABILITY CENTERS FOR YOUNG ADULTS AGES 18 AND ABOVE

College or Center	Remediation and Training	For Information Contact
ALABAMA		
Brewer State Junior College (2 yr.)	Open-door policy with placement tests. Specialized programs in math, English, reading, and study skills.	Jerre Strickland Developmental Education Program Brewer State Junior College Fayette, Ala. 35555
Daniel Payne College (4 yr.)	Individualized instruction and counseling. Developmental study skills program.	Ms. Rea Trennen Title III Coordinator Daniel Payne College 2101 West Sayreton Road Birmingham, Ala. 35214
Patrick Henry State Junior College (2 yr.)	Individualized teaching and counseling. Developmental studies are taught to find areas of disabilities.	John Lamkin Patrick Henry State Junior College Box 731 Monroeville, Ala. 36460
S. D. Bishop State Junior College (2 yr.)	Tutorial activities by students and staff. Developmental reading program. College premath. Special basic freshman program.	Mrs. M. Y. Dillard Registrar S. D. Bishop State Junior College 351 North Broad Street Mobile, Ala. 36603

Selma University (2 yr. & 4 yr.)	Formal instruction. Individual and group tutoring. Small reading groups. Students repeat courses until a satisfactory score is made.	Mrs. Ira M. Durgan Director, Student Support and Special Program Selma University Selma, Ala. 36701

ALASKA

	Not given	Gloria D. Oakes President Alaska ACLD 7420 Old Harbor Avenue Anchorage, Alaska 99504

ARIZONA

Navajo Community College (2 yr.)	Small classes. Teaching on a one-to-one basis. Directed studies program. Remediation according to need.	Mary L. Pettit Director, Special Education Navajo Community College Tsaile, Ariz. 86556
Scottsdale Community College (2 yr.)	Developmental English and reading programs.	Dr. Glenn Groenke Chairman, Communications Studies Scottsdale Community College P.O. Box Y Scottsdale, Ariz. 85251

ARKANSAS

College of the Ozarks	Not given	C. Douglas Saddler, Ph.D. Director, Special Learning Center College of the Ozarks Clarksville, Ark. 72830

LEARNING DISABLITY CENTERS FOR YOUNG ADULTS AGES 18 AND ABOVE—CONTINUED

College or Center	Remediation and Training	For Information Contact
CALIFORNIA		
Bakersfield College (2 yr.)	Special classwork; self-paced courses, workbooks, programmed learning.	Director of Counseling Office of Student Services Bakersfield College 1801 Panorama Drive Bakersfield, Calif. 93305
California State University, Northridge (4 yr.)	Applicants must meet minimum admissions requirements. Special services to support academic experience. Tutors available. Library study facility available.	Jean Hutchinson Assistant to the Dean Admissions and Records California State University Northridge, Calif. 91324
Child Improvement Center	Classroom skills and social interaction included in the special education program. Saturday tutoring program available. Work-training and job-placement programs available.	Larry Neese Director Child Improvement Center 6351 Hood Avenue Huntington Park, Calif. 91255
College of the Redwoods (2 yr.)	Programmed learning. Tutorials. Mediated instruction.	Dean Carl Lude Student Special Services College of the Redwoods Eureka, Calif. 95501

Devereux Foundation	Work training, job-skill building, vocational rehabilitation, remedial school.	Keith A. Seaton Admissions Officer The Devereux Foundation in California P.O. Box 1079 Santa Barbara, Calif. 93102
Merced College (2 yr.)	Self-paced instruction, tutoring. Course-work modification, individual counseling.	Lynn Ireland Program for Handicapped Merced College 3600 M Street Merced, Calif. 95340
Mira Costa College (2 yr.)	Reading labs, remediation, special tutorial offered.	Paul H. Schoenbeck Director, Education Priorities Center Mira Costa College One Barnard Drive Oceanside, Calif. 92054
Southwestern College (2 yr.)	Remedial courses focusing on basic skills. Small group instruction. Diagnostic clinic and learning specialists employed.	Leon L. Stewart Counseling Southwestern College 900 Otay Lakes Road Chula Vista, Calif. 92010

LEARNING DISABLITY CENTERS FOR YOUNG ADULTS AGES 18 AND ABOVE—CONTINUED

COLLEGE OR CENTER	REMEDIATION AND TRAINING	FOR INFORMATION CONTACT
COLORADO		
Adams State College (4 yr.)	Basic-skills lab, reading lab, tutorial assistance.	Neva Harden Division of Humanities Adams State College Alamosa, Colo. 81102
El Paso Community College (2 yr.)	Reading, data processing, machining, food preservation, tutorial assistance.	Dr. Steven H. Walker Coordinator, Handicapped Program El Paso Community College 2200 Bott Avenue Colorado Springs, Colo. 80904
Lamar Community College (2 yr.)	Prescriptive education, special tutorial and other programs.	Elaine Noccarato Prescriptive Education Lamar Community College Lamar, Colo. 81052
Mesa College (4 yr., 2 yr., post h.s.)	Tutorials, remedial reading and math. Special clerical program. Special programs in auto mechanics, welding, and body and fender work.	Robert Stokes Mesa College 1120 North Avenue Grand Junction, Colo. 81501

Morgan Community College (2 yr.)	Special program called "College for Living"	Janna Thiel Morgan Community College 300 Main Street Fort Morgan, Colo. 80701

CONNECTICUT

Annhurst College	Not given	Kathy Jane Garretson Director, The Learning Center Annhurst College R.R. #2 Woodstock, Conn. 06281
The Foundation School	Individualized program with team teaching approach. Special services (e.g., language training, perceptual motor training) available. Manual arts and shop. on-job training.	Walter J. Bell Executive Director The Foundation School 719 Derby-Milford Road Orange, Conn. 06477

DELAWARE

Wesley College	Not given	Dr. Presley Hayes Director of Counseling Wesley College Dover, Del. 19901

LEARNING DISABLITY CENTERS FOR YOUNG ADULTS AGES 18 AND ABOVE—CONTINUED

COLLEGE OR CENTER	REMEDIATION AND TRAINING	FOR INFORMATION CONTACT
DISTRICT OF COLUMBIA		
Howard University (4 yr.)	Program involves counseling, math, and verbal development. Systematic instruction in small groups with independent laboratory activities.	Dr. Eunice S. Newton The Center for Academic Reinforcement Howard University 2400 Sixth Street, NW Washington, D.C. 20059
Southeastern University	Courses offered within the Division of Educational Development and Research for students.	B. D. McDowell Southeastern University 501 Eye Street, SW Washington, D.C. 20024
FLORIDA		
Barry College (4 yr.)	Reading and tutoring programs.	Dr. A. Sutton Center for Learning Disabilities Barry College 11300 NE Second Avenue Miami, Fla. 33161
Central Florida Community College (2 yr.)	Individual instruction, lab work, remedial program, tutorial assistance.	Carolyn West Central Florida Community College Box 1388 Ocala, Fla. 32670

234

GEORGIA

Academy of Professional Drafting	Individualized oral instruction. Math, reading, study skills.	Vida G. Roberts Director Academy of Professional Drafting 1655 Peachtree Street, NE Atlanta, Ga. 30338
Andrew College (2 yr.)	Placed in regular classes with individualized attention and special tutoring.	Morris G. Raye Dean of Admissions College Street Andrew College Cuthbert, Ga. 31740
Georgia Southwestern College (4 yr.)	Developmental studies program. Remedial courses, counseling and testing offered.	James M. Robbins Assistant Registrar Georgia Southwestern College Americus, Ga. 31709

HAWAII

	Not given	Mrs. Phyllis Rice President Hawaii ACLD 2877 Kalakua 107 Honolulu, Hawaii 96815

IDAHO

College of Southern Idaho	Individualized instruction, study skills center.	Marvin Glasscock College of Southern Idaho Twin Falls, Idaho 83301

LEARNING DISABLITY CENTERS FOR YOUNG ADULTS AGES 18 AND ABOVE—CONTINUED

COLLEGE OR CENTER	REMEDIATION AND TRAINING	FOR INFORMATION CONTACT
Lewis-Clark State College (4 yr.)	Work on study skills. Remedial center.	Earl A. Loomis Lewis-Clark State College Lewiston, Idaho 83501
ILLINOIS		
Kendall College (2 yr.)	Individualized instruction.	Karen Anderson Director of Admissions Kendall College 2408 Orrington Evanston, Ill. 60204
Lincoln College (2 yr.)	Individualized program with one-to-one instruction. Special testing and diagnosis program.	Dean of Admissions Lincoln College Lincoln, Ill. 62656
Moraine Valley Community College	Exceptional education program to train paraprofessionals for work with handicapped children and adults.	Judith Mitzner Exceptional Education Coordinator Moraine Valley Community College 10900 South Eighty-eighth Avenue Palos Hills, Ill. 60465
Parkland College (2 yr.)	Activities and methods prescribed on basis of student needs and diagnostic workup. Individualized program, learning lab.	Louella Snyder Learning Lab Parkland College 2400 West Bradley Champagne, Ill. 61820

INDIANA

Institution	Description	Contact
University of Evansville	Not given	Director of Program Coordination University of Evansville 500 Second Avenue Evansville, Ind. 47710

IOWA

Institution	Description	Contact
Coe College	Reading and writing laboratory. Regular tutoring in specific course areas.	Alan B. McIvor Office of Admissions Coe College Cedar Rapids, Iowa 52402
Sioux Empire College (2 yr.)	Classwork with individual tutors, self-paced.	Dr. A. D. Hudek Sioux Empire College Box 312 Hawarden, Iowa 51023
Waldorf College (2 yr.)	Individualized attention. Limited load. Special tutoring available.	Ken Johnson Waldorf College Forest City, Iowa 50436

KANSAS

Institution	Description	Contact
Kansas Newman College (4 yr.)	Developmental courses and weekly small group meetings. Workshops offered in study skills, job applications, and vocational guidance. Aptitude testing and career orientation.	Sister Aegidia Werth Education Lab 3100 McCormick Kansas Newman College Wichita, Kans. 67213

LEARNING DISABLITY CENTERS FOR YOUNG ADULTS
AGES 18 AND ABOVE—CONTINUED

College or Center	Remediation and Training	For Information Contact
Kansas Technical Institute	Provides remedial math and English programs. Learning center.	Charles P. Scott Director, Office of Student Affairs Kansas Technical Institute 2409 Scanlan Avenue Salina, Kans. 67401
KENTUCKY		
Charles L. Shedd APSL Research Academy	Individualized curriculum. Residential and day programs. Occupational therapy.	Philip Parker, Head Charles L. Shedd APSL Learning Academy 214 South Eighth Street P.O. Box 259 Mayfield, Ky. 42066
Kentucky State University (4 yr.)	Special programs. Reading and Study Skills Center.	Mrs. Hattie Duncan Director of Special Services Kentucky State University Frankfort, Ky. 40601
LOUISIANA		
Louisiana Polytechnic Institute	Training and curriculum levels vary with project objectives.	Department of Special Education Louisiana Polytechnic Institute Box 5857, Tech. Station Ruston, La. 71270

Institution	Services	Contact
University of Southwestern Louisiana (4 yr.)	Special arrangements made in individual cases. Remedial work and tutoring available.	Mr. James Caillier Director, Special Services Program University of Southwestern Louisiana Lafayette, La. 70501

MAINE

Institution	Services	Contact
University of Maine—Farmington	Extensive support services offered. Special tutor assigned to monitor student progress.	Ed Nunery Program of Basic Studies University of Maine—Farmington 85 Main Street Farmington, Maine 04938
University of Maine—Augusta (2 yr.)	Special remedial course work offered. Audiovisual input. Programmed learning concept. Individual pace—criterion-referenced units.	Frank J. Antonucci University Counseling Center University of Maine—Augusta Augusta, Maine 04330

MARYLAND

Institution	Services	Contact
Community College of Baltimore (2 yr.)	Remedial courses, extended time, tutorial and laboratory opportunities.	Marvin Davis Developmental Studies Community College of Baltimore 2901 Liberty Heights Avenue Baltimore, Md. 21215
Frostburg State College (4 yr.)	Tutoring, study skills, courses, and academic advisement available. Special student services.	Director, Student Special Services 207 Dunkle Hall Frostburg State College Frostburg, Md. 21532

239

LEARNING DISABLITY CENTERS FOR YOUNG ADULTS
AGES 18 AND ABOVE—CONTINUED

College or Center	Remediation and Training	For Information Contact
MASSACHUSETTS		
Curry College (4 yr.)	Support program rather than modification. Textbooks on tape. Supportive counseling available.	Professor Gertrude M. Webb Curry College Learning Center Milton, Mass. 02186
North Adams State College	Work on one-to-one basis with each individual. Skills development program to aid and assist each student.	Charlotte Degen Skills Center North Adams State College North Adams, Mass. 01247
MICHIGAN		
Andrews University (4 yr.)	Remedial reading if needed, and special course in "How to Study."	Mrs. Marion Swanepoel Director of Freshman Activities Andrews University Counseling & Testing Berrien Springs, Mich. 49104
Spring Arbor College (4 yr.)	Reading. Study skills, counseling offered.	Charles Campbell Freshman Program Spring Arbor College Spring Arbor, Mich. 49283
University of Michigan, Dearborn (4 yr.)	Special project program—reading skill program.	Dr. Don Brown Assistant Director, Counseling Division University of Michigan 4901 Evergreen Road Dearborn, Mich. 48128

MINNESOTA

Minneapolis Drafting School	Noncompetitive programmed learning. Individual instruction. Varied employment levels.	Robert Casserly Director MPLS Drafting School 3407 Chicago Avenue Minneapolis, Minn. 55407
Normandale Community College (2 yr.)	Developmental studies program to meet individual students' needs.	Dr. John L. Hilborn Dean of Students Normandale Community College 9700 France Avenue S Bloomington, Minn. 55431
University of Minnesota, Duluth	Courses selected from regular curriculum according to individual needs. Supportive services provided.	Dr. H. Brenden Director, Supportive Services Program University of Minnesota, Duluth Duluth, Minn. 55804

MISSISSIPPI

Whitmore College (4 yr.)	Faculty works directly with each student or small group.	Mrs. Ira Mayfield Whitmore College Brookhaven, Miss. 39601
William Carey College (4 yr.)	Not given	Antonio R. Pascals Director of Admissions William Carey College Hattiesburg, Miss. 39401

241

LEARNING DISABLITY CENTERS FOR YOUNG ADULTS AGES 18 AND ABOVE—CONTINUED

COLLEGE OR CENTER	REMEDIATION AND TRAINING	FOR INFORMATION CONTACT
MISSOURI		
Mackler Professional Tutors	Program tailored to need and learning style of student. Career counseling.	Leona Mackler Mackler Professional Tutors 8420 Delmar University City, Mo. 63124
Missouri Baptist College	Flexible time blocks are designated for completing program.	Registrar Missouri Baptist College 12542 Conway Road Creve Coeur, Mo. 63141
Missouri Western State College	Remedial courses offered. Learning skills center to aid in reading, writing, and comprehension skills.	Dr. George Richmond Chairman, Department of Elementary Education Missouri Western State College St. Joseph, Mo. 64507
MONTANA		
Great Falls Commercial College	All materials are programmed for individual progress. Tutorial program.	Denis Wingen Director, Ebronix Learning Center Great Falls Commercial College 905 First Avenue N Great Falls, Mont. 59403

NEBRASKA

Doane College (4 yr.)	Not given	Susan Snow Reading and Learning Center Doane College Crete, Nebraska 68333

NEVADA

	Not given	Ms. Theresa Smith President, Nevada ACLD 4034 South Great Plains Way Las Vegas, Nev. 89121

NEW HAMPSHIRE

Hesser College (2 yr.)	Study skills, business skills courses. Individual and tutorial attention.	J. Donovan Mills Director of Admissions Hesser College 155 Concord Street Manchester, N.H. 03103
New Hampshire School of Electronics and Commerce, Inc.	All work on one-to-one basis. Practical trade training for job entry.	Socrates Chaloge President New Hampshire School of Electronics and Commerce, Inc. 359 Franklin Street Manchester, N.H. 03101

LEARNING DISABLITY CENTERS FOR YOUNG ADULTS AGES 18 AND ABOVE—CONTINUED

College or Center	Remediation and Training	For Information Contact
New Hampshire Vocational-Technical College, Nashua (2 yr.)	Not given	Robert E. Bloomfield Director New Hampshire Vocational-Technical College 505 Amherst Street Nashua, N.H. 03060
NEW JERSEY		
Bloomfield College	Special programs.	Peter Scudder Bloomfield College Bloomfield, N.J. 07003
Jersey State College	Special curriculum and faculty.	Dr. Gary Spencer Director, Learning Center Jersey State College Jersey City, N.J. 07305
NEW MEXICO		
New Mexico Institute of Mining and Technology (4 yr.)	Small classes, individual tutors. Special summer programs.	Simon J. Gormuki Director of Admissions and Financial Aids New Mexico Institute of Mining and Technology Socorro, N. Mex. 87801

Southwest College	Individualized remedial program designed to make the individual employable in the shortest possible time.	Jo-Ann K. Bloom Southwest College 525 San Pedro, NE Albuquerque, N. Mex. 87108

NEW YORK

Berk Trade School	Not given	E. Kelfer Berk Trade School 384 Atlantic Avenue Brooklyn, N.Y. 11217
Eastern School for Physicians' Aides	Some courses are specializations within the larger medical lab technician courses and can accommodate the LD student.	Mr. Wm. Schafer Eastern School for Physicians' Aides 85 Fifth Avenue New York, N.Y. 10003
Jefferson Community College (2 yr.)	Special courses, individualized instruction, team teaching, vocational guidance.	John G. Phillips Jefferson Community College P.O. Box 473 Watertown, N.Y. 13601
The Karafin School, Inc.	Special materials, machines, texts as well as methodology used.	Dr. Albert I. Karafin The Karafin School 111 Radio Circle Mount Kisco, N.Y. 10549

NORTH CAROLINA

Lenoir Community College	Not given	Dr. Ben Spangler Director of Counseling Services Lenoir Community College Kinston, N.C. 28501

LEARNING DISABILITY CENTERS FOR YOUNG ADULTS AGES 18 AND ABOVE—CONTINUED

College or Center	Remediation and Training	For Information Contact
National School of Heavy Equipment	Not given	Gene M. Collins National School of Heavy Equipment P.O. Box 8529 Charlotte, N.C. 28208
NORTH DAKOTA		
Hanson Mechanical Trade School	Not given	Ansel O. Hakanson Hanson Mechanical Trade School Box 1780 65 Third Street N Fargo, N. Dak. 58102
North Dakota State School of Science (2 yr.)	Students may receive individualized or small group tutoring.	James Horton Director, Learning Skills Center North Dakota State School of Science Wahpeton, N. Dak. 58075
OHIO		
Ohio State University	Students placed under Freshman Foundations program receiving tutoring and special services.	William A. Fulghum Disability Services Ohio State University 154 West Twelfth Avenue Columbus, Ohio 43210

Wright State University	Not given	Dean of Admissions Wright State University W. 475B Millett Hall Dayton, Ohio 45431

OKLAHOMA

Oklahoma Baptist University (4 yr.)	Not given	Paul Travis Director, Trio Programs Oklahoma Baptist University Shawnee, Okla. 74801
Oklahoma State Tech.	Not given	Registrar's Office Oklahoma State Tech. Okmulgee, Okla. 74447

OREGON

Central Oregon Community College (2 yr.)	Developmental program in math, English, and reading.	R. R. Meddish Registrar Central Oregon Community College Bend, Oreg. 97701
Lane Community College (2 yr.)	Small group and one-to-one instruction. Emphasis on skill mastery.	Jim Ellison Study Skills Learning Center Lane Community College 4000 East Thirtieth Avenue Eugene, Oreg. 97401

LEARNING DISABILITY CENTERS FOR YOUNG ADULTS AGES 18 AND ABOVE—CONTINUED

College or Center	Remediation and Training	For Information Contact
PENNSYLVANIA		
American Institute of Drafting	All work on an individual basis. Program modifications to meet special students' needs.	Sam King American Institute of Drafting 1616 Orthodox Street Philadelphia, Pa. 19124
New Castle Business College	Lab classes and individual instruction. Tutoring available. Testing and individual scheduling. Remedial classes and special study lab.	Mr. Samuel Haycock New Castle Business College 316 Rhodes Place New Castle, Pa. 16101
Seton Hill College (4 yr.)	Special counseling and tutorial program. Summer tutorial help and cultural assistance. Career counseling.	Sister Jean Boggs Seton Hill College Greensburg, Pa. 15601
RHODE ISLAND		
University of Rhode Island (4 yr.)	Reduced student academic load. Help in study skills.	Marcus Rand Assistant Director of Admissions University of Rhode Island Kingston, R.I. 02881
SOUTH CAROLINA		
Counseling Center	Clinical curriculum that includes tutoring. Prescriptive teaching techniques. Faculty-student ratio of one to one.	Counseling Center 114 Kuker Ave. Florence, S.C. 29501

SOUTH DAKOTA

College		Contact
Mount Marty College (4 yr.)	No special classes. Individual attention provided.	J. Patrick Merrigan Director of Admissions Mount Marty College Yankton, S. Dak. 57078
National College of Business (2 yr. & 4 yr.)	Much remedial work is programmed for those needing such help.	Guy Tillett National College of Business Box 1780 Rapid City, S. Dak. 57701

TENNESSEE

College		Contact
Tennessee Institute of Electronics	Not given	E. R. Massengill Tennessee Institute of Electronics 3121 Broadway, NE Knoxville, Tenn. 37917
University of Tennessee	Reading center, rehabilitation counselor, advising counseling center, and other special services.	Assistant Dean of Admissions University of Tennessee 305 Student Services Building Knoxville, Tenn. 37916

TEXAS

College		Contact
American Technological University (4 yr.)	Classes scheduled to meet student needs.	Ron Meek Director of Admissions American Technological University P.O. Box 1416 Killeen, Tex. 76541

249

LEARNING DISABLITY CENTERS FOR YOUNG ADULTS
AGES 18 AND ABOVE—CONTINUED

College or Center	Remediation and Training	For Information Contact
Gulf Coast Bible College (4 yr.)	Remedial courses. Certificates given in lieu of degrees.	W. Maurice Slater Director of Admissions Gulf Coast Bible College 911 West Eleventh Street Houston, Tex. 77008
Mountain View College (2 yr.)	Special assistance provided. Multimodal emphasis on language dysfunction. Learning skills center.	Louise H. Miller Director, Human Development Center Mountain View College 4849 West Illinois Dallas, Tex. 75211
Tarrant County Junior College (2 yr.)	Three programs available: drafting, secretarial, and TV & radio repair. Emphasis is on skill development. Many support services provided.	Joan Fernades S.C.O.O.P. Tarrant County Junior College Northeast Campus 828 Harwood Road Hurst, Tex. 76053
Texas State Technical Institute, James Connally Campus	Individualized, self-paced instruction. Open learning labs using multimedia approach. Remedial center for prevocational development.	Mr. W. G. Rueter Pretechnical Studies James Connally Campus Texas State Technical Institute Waco, Tex. 75211

Texas State Technical Institute, Rio Grande Campus	Special curriculum, regular vocational program.	Gene Campos Texas State Technical Institute P.O. Box 2628 Harlingen, Tex. 78550
University of Plano (4 yr.)	Special courses individually geared to the student. The Doman and Delacato methods employed.	Mrs. Barbara Goostree Director, Middle College Program University of Plano Drawer 418 Plano, Tex. 75074

UTAH

	Not given	Mrs. Lee Zumbrunnen President Utah ACLD 1806 East 3780 S Salt Lake City, Utah 84106

VERMONT

Johnson State College (4 yr.)	Skills development, study habit development, tutorial assistance, and academic or personal counseling.	David A. Crary Johnson State College Johnson, Vt. 05656
Southern Vermont College (2 yr. & 4 yr.)	Adviser/tutor program. Individualized instruction.	Mr. James G. Donahue President Southern Vermont College Monument Road Bennington, Vt. 05201

LEARNING DISABLITY CENTERS FOR YOUNG ADULTS AGES 18 AND ABOVE—CONTINUED

College or Center	Remediation and Training	For Information Contact
Ver-shire Schools and Shops	Individualized programing and tutoring.	George Coulter NKMHS, Inc. 60 Broadview Avenue Newport, Vt. 05855
VIRGINIA		
Broadcast Academy of Richmond, Inc.	Students work at their own pace. Classes or private tutoring.	Karen Myers Broadcast Academy of Richmond, Inc. Suite 200 2120 Staples Mill Road Richmond, Va. 23230
Dabney S. Lancaster Community College (2 yr.)	Self-paced instruction, tutoring, special materials and equipment.	Mr. Colin Ferguson Developmental Studies Division Dabney S. Lancaster Community College Clifton Forge, Va. 24422
Southern Virginia Community College (2 yr.)	Remedial courses aimed toward correction of weaknesses and emphasizing strengths.	Mr. John Sykes Southern Virginia Community College Alberta, Va. 23821

WASHINGTON

Fort Steilacoom Community College (2 yr.)	Tutors, individual study, programmed learning, career educations.	Pearl Rose Occupational Education Office Fort Steilacoom Community College P.O. Box 99186 Tacoma, Wash. 98499
Shoreline Community College (2 yr.)	Individualized instruction, independent living. Nurse's aide, foods, clerical training.	Mrs. Willamay Pym Shoreline Community College 16101 Greenwood Avenue N Seattle, Wash. 98133
Walla Walla Community College (2 yr.)	Individualized instruction.	Mrs. Hilda Thompson Coordinator of Developmental Education Walla Walla Community College 500 Tausick Way Walla Walla, Wash. 99362

WEST VIRGINIA

Mountain State College (2 yr.)	Individualized instruction.	Bert L. Walter Mountain State College 1508 Spring Street Parkersburg, W. Va. 26101
West Virginia State College	Individualized instruction.	Nelson R. Bickle Director, Guidance & Placement West Virginia State College Institute, W. Va. 25112

LEARNING DISABILITY CENTERS FOR YOUNG ADULTS
AGES 18 AND ABOVE—CONTINUED

College or Center	Remediation and Training	For Information Contact
WISCONSIN		
Lakeland College	Not given	Director of Admissions Lakeland College Sheboygan, Wis. 53081
University of Wisconsin, Oshkosh (4 yr.)	Mediated, self-paced instruction, tutoring, clinical services. Flexible programming. Associate degrees.	New Student Center University of Wisconsin, Oshkosh Oshkosh, Wis. 54901
WYOMING		
Central Wyoming College (2 yr.)	Individualized instruction.	Warren Cole Central Wyoming College Riverton, Wyo. 82501

BIBLIOGRAPHY

CHAPTER 1

Abraham, W. "The Slow Learner—Surrounded and Alone." *Today's Health* 43 (March 1965): 40–41.

Barsch, R. H. *Achieving Perceptual-Motor Efficiency.* Seattle, Wash.: Special Child Publications, 1967, chap. 9.

Binet, A. "The Development of the Binet-Simon Scale." In *The Causes of Behavior*, by J. F. Rosenblith and W. Allensmith. Boston: Allyn & Bacon, 1962.

Birch, H. G., ed. *Brain Damage in Children.* Baltimore: Williams & Wilkins, 1964.

Cruickshank, W. M. "Learning Disabilities: Perceptual or Other?" *ACLD Newsbrief*, March/April 1979.

Eisenberg, L. "Behavioral Manifestations of Cerebral Damage in Childhood." In *Brain Damage in Children*, edited by H. G. Birch. Baltimore: Williams & Wilkins, 1964.

Gesell, A., *The First Five Years of Life* (Part One). New York: Harper & Brothers, 1940.

Hagin, R. A., and Silver, A. A. "Learning Disability: Definition, Diagnosis, and Prevention." New York University's *Education Quarterly*, Winter 1977.

Ingram, C. P. *Education of the Slow-Learning Child.* New York: Ronald Press, 1960.

Johnson, D. J., and Myklebust, H. R. *Learning Disabilities.* New York: Grune & Stratton, 1971.

Johnson, G. O. *Education for the Slow Learners.* Englewood Cliffs, N.J.: Prentice-Hall, 1963.

Knobloch, H., and Pasamanick, B. *Gesell and Amatruda's Developmental Diagnosis.* New York: Harper & Row, 1974.

Kranes, J. E. "Intelligence and Creativity." *New Perceptions of Children's Behavior and Needs.* Child Study Association of America, March 5, 1963.

Langer, S. *Philosophy in a New Key.* Cambridge, Mass.: Harvard University Press, 1957.

Lewis, R. S. *The Other Child Grows Up.* New York: The New York Times Book Co., 1977.

Mayman, M.; Schafer, R.; and Rapaport, D. "General Intelligence Tests in Personality Appraisal." In *Projective Techniques*, by H. H. Anderson and G. L. Anderson. New York: Prentice-Hall, 1951.

Piaget, J. *Judgement and Reasoning in the Child*. New York: Harcourt Brace, 1928.

———. *The Psychology of Intelligence*. New York: Harcourt Brace, 1950.

Sarason, S., and Doris, J. "Public Law 94-142: What Does It Say?" *The Exceptional Parent*, August 1977.

Siegel, E. *The Exceptional Child Grows Up*. New York: E. P. Dutton, 1975.

CHAPTER 2

Beck, J. *How to Raise a Brighter Child*. New York: Simon and Schuster, 1967.

Chaney, C. M., and Kephart, N. C. *Motoric Aids to Perceptual Training*. Columbus, Ohio: Charles E. Merrill, 1968.

Draper, M. W., and Draper, H. E. *Caring for Children*. Peoria, Ill.: Charles A. Bennett, 1969.

Elkind, D. "Giant in the Nursery—Jean Piaget." *The New York Times Magazine*, May 26, 1968.

Hunt, J. McV. *Intelligence and Experience*. New York: Ronald Press, 1961.

Isaacs, N. *New Light on Children's Ideas of Number*. London: Ward Lock Educational Co., 1968.

Johnson, D. J., and Myklebust, H. R. *Learning Disabilities*. New York: Grune & Stratton, 1971.

Johnson, G. O. *Education for the Slow Learners*. Englewood Cliffs, N.J.: Prentice-Hall, 1963.

Keller, H. *The Story of My Life*. New York: Doubleday, 1905.

Neill, A. S. *Summerhill*. New York: Hart Publishing, 1963.

Sarason, S. B., and Gladwin, T. G. *Psychological Problems in Mental Deficiency*. 3d. ed. New York: Harper & Brothers, 1959.

Snitzer, H. *Living at Summerhill*. New York: Collier Books, 1969.

White, B. L. *The First Three Years of Life*. New York: Avon Books, 1978.

CHAPTER 3

Church, J. *Language and the Discovery of Reality*. New York: Random House, 1961.

Draper, M. W., and Draper, H. E. *Caring for Children*. Peoria, Ill.: Charles A. Bennett, 1969.

Elkind, D. "Giant in the Nursery—Jean Piaget." *The New York Times Magazine*, May 26, 1968.

Fraiberg, S. H. *The Magic Years*. New York: Charles Scribner's Sons, 1959.

Gesell, A. and Ilg, F. M. *The Child from Five to Ten*. New York: Harper & Brothers, 1946.

Isaacs, N. *New Light on Children's Ideas of Number*. London: Ward Lock Educational Co., 1968.

Knobloch, H., and Pasamanick, B. *Gesell and Amatruda's Developmental Diagnosis*. New York: Harper & Row, 1974.

Schneider, H., and Schneider, N. *Science for Here and Now*. Lexington, Mass.: D. C. Heath, 1973.

Spencer, P. L., and Brydegaard, M. *Building Mathematical Concepts in the Elementary School*. New York: Henry Holt, 1956.

Stone, L. J., and Church, J. *Childhood and Adolescence*. New York: Random House, 1957.

Vernon, J. A.; McGill, T. W.; Gulick, W. C.; and Candland, D. "The Effect of Human Isolation upon Some Perceptual and Motor Skills." In *Sensory Deprivation*, edited by P. Solomon. Cambridge, Mass.: Harvard University Press, 1961.

White, B. L. *The First Three Years of Life*. New York: Avon Books, 1978.

CHAPTER 4

Bureau of Elementary Curriculum Development. *The Elementary School Curriculum: An Overview*. New York State Education Department, 1954.

Burrows, A. T.; Monson, D. L.; Stauffer, R. G. *New Horizons in the Language Arts*. New York: Harper & Row, 1972.

Ingram, C. P. *Education of the Slow-Learning Child*. New York: Ronald Press, 1960.

Schneider, H., and Schneider, N. *Science for Here and Now*. Lexington, Mass.: D. C. Heath, 1973.

Spencer, P. L., and Brydegaard, M. *Building Mathematical Concepts in the Elementary School*. New York: Henry Holt, 1956.

Stone, L. J., and Church, J. *Childhood and Adolescence*. New York: Random House, 1957.

Strickland, R. G. *The Language Arts in the Elementary School*. Boston: D. C. Heath, 1951.

Young, M. A. *Teaching Children with Special Learning Needs*. New York: John Day, 1967.

CHAPTER 5

Elkind, D. "Giant in the Nursery—Jean Piaget." *The New York Times Magazine*, May 26, 1968.

Schneider, H., and Schneider, N. *Science Far and Near*. Lexington, Mass.: D. C. Heath, 1973.

CHAPTER 7

Eisenberg, L. "Behavior Manifestations of Cerebral Damage in Childhood." In *Brain Damage in Children*, ed. by H. G. Birch. New York: Williams & Wilkins, 1964.

Gordon, S. "Marriage and Parenting." *Exceptional Children*, April 1977.

Johnson, D. J., and Myklebust, H. R. *Learning Disabilities*. New York: Grune & Stratton, 1971.

Knobloch, H., and Pasamanick, B. *Gesell and Amatruda's Developmental Diagnosis*. New York: Harper & Row, 1974.

Sarason, S. G., and Gladwin, T. G. *Psychological Problems in Mental Deficiency*, 3d ed. New York: Harper & Brothers, 1959.

INDEX

Index

phone book, 182–83
physical ability, 31, 97
physical development, 57, 58,
  82, 99
Piaget, Jean, 38, 57, 78, 81–82,
  84
Pierce, Opal, 12
Pinkerton Foundation, 11
plants, 111–12, 156, 179–80
play, 94–103
  aggressiveness in, 94–95, 99
  competitiveness in, 94, 101
  "free" play, 99–100
  games, 100–101, 120–23,
    130, 134, 223
  imagination in, 102
  materials and equipment, 88,
    93, 96–98, 102, 223–24
  role acting, 102–3
  team play, 100–101
politics in education of
  handicapped, 48, 52
Pope, Prof. Lillie, 13
problem solving, 33, 57–58, 64,
  100, 135, 149, 152, 153,
  181
proverbs, 59
punishment, 95

Ralph, 199–203
readiness for learning, 65–66
reading, 35, 45, 113–16, 182
regularity, 91–92
  see also routine and schedule
retarded, 27–32, 40, 49–51,
  167, 169, 176, 219
Rich, Miss, 205
Ringelheim, Prof. Daniel, 13
Riva, 186
Riverside Nursery-
  Kindergarten, 12

Rodney, Miss, 178
role playing, 94, 101–3
Roman, Mrs., 137
routine and schedule, 51, 90–
  92, 184, 225

St. Luke's Nursery School, 12
Salvation Army, 12, 218
Salwyn, Mrs., 93
Sarason, Dr. Seymour, 47,
  214
Sargent, J. Kathryn, 226
Saturday Review, 26
Sawhill, John C., 17
Schneider Science Series, 118
Schwartz, Judith, 11–12
Schwyzer, Kathryn, 12
segregation, 52
  see also mainstreaming
self-confidence, 80, 92–93,
  140, 219
self-control, 94–96
Sema, 39–40
Senden, Mrs., 98
sensitivity period, 66
sensory-motor activities, 57,
  79, 101
sensory organs, 159–60
sex education, 209–13
shapes, 152, 153
Shapiro, Leo, 12
shopping, 124, 127
Silver, Dr. Achie, 46
Simon, Dr. Ann, 12
Skinner, Burrhus F., 56
slow learners, 15, 25, 27, 31,
  32, 47–52, 66–67, 166–
  169
  definition of, 25
  literature on, 196
  mental-growth chart, 66